Action-Centred Leadership

Other McGraw-Hill books of related interest

Action-Centred Leadership

John *Eric* Adair

London · New York · St Louis · San Francisco · Düsseldorf
Johannesburg · Kuala Lumpur · Mexico · Montreal · New Delhi
Panama · Paris · São Paulo · Singapore · Sydney · Toronto

Published by

McGRAW-HILL Book Company (UK) Limited

Maidenhead · Berkshire · England

---

07 084428 3

PRINTED AND BOUND IN GREAT BRITAIN

Contents

Introduction

The aim of this book is to present to the reader a wide spectrum of experience in the application of Action-Centred Leadership (ACL) training to the different needs of organizations. Besides illustrating and confirming the value of this particular approach towards developing management potential, it is hoped that the following chapters will also serve as a guidebook for those wishing to improve the effectiveness of the leadership in their organizations along ACL lines.

The apparent emphasis on the word 'leadership' may cause some initial disquiet. In the first chapter, however, its meaning is carefully defined in order to preclude the possibility of any misunderstanding. But in the last analysis it is not the word that matters, but the reality to which it points. Most reactions against the word 'leader' are really directed against bad leadership, in one or both of the double senses of the word 'bad', namely, (1) inappropriate to the general situation, or (2) directed towards less than moral ends. There is now a much greater recognition that if democracy is to progress and if organizations within free societies are to press forward towards the fulfilment of their purposes in the increasingly complex social conditions of the next decade, then good leadership of a quality and in a quantity previously unknown is already urgently required. This book relates and documents a major training approach towards developing such leadership.

The short leadership training course described, discussed, and evaluated in these pages took shape at the Royal Military Academy, Sandhurst, between 1962 and 1964 as a part of an overall programme for developing the potential in officer cadets whose average age was 18 to 20 years. In 1964, when adopting it as their basic approach, the Royal Air Force called it Functional Leadership.

Four years later, the Industrial Society entitled this approach Action-Centred Leadership (ACL). Although this name has the advantage that it highlights the emphasis within this form of training on what the leader *does* rather than upon what he has to *be*, nevertheless it has received some criticism as sounding too much like a gimmick and for not adequately describing the theory and content of the approach, which is very much more than a management training 'package'. In the following pages some of the contributors have not only shown how the suggested course can be used flexibly in a variety of ways, but they have not hesitated to give it new names or no name at all, a freedom which is open to all users of ACL subject only to the normal laws of copyright. The initials ACL are now so widely known and convenient, however, that they appear frequently below.

In chapter one I have outlined fully the research and general concepts upon which ACL rests. The educational philosophy and training methods employed in evolving the course at Sandhurst have already been fully described in my book *Training for Leadership* (1968). But it might be convenient for the reader if I recapitulate the salient points.

In order to improve the effectiveness of leadership development in any organization it was suggested that five *areas* should be closely considered. Firstly, the *structure* of the organization should allow plenty of opportunities for the practice of leadership under varying degrees of supervision; and the climate and organizational values, often summed up in the word 'tradition', should encourage and foster the deeper attitudes of good leadership. Secondly, both the content and the methods of the *formal* or explicit instruction on leadership should be of the highest quality. Thirdly, such course work should be related to the opportunities for *practical leadership training* afforded elsewhere in the training programme. Fourthly, *staff* members should have the chance to study and improve their performance in the role of leadership trainers; and lastly, a small *research and advisory team* is absolutely essential to maintain and improve standards. It was recognized that the scope for developments in these five areas depended very much upon the nature and situation of the organization in question.

Within the control of the second area—the explicit training course—the key to learning lay in the dialogue between theory and practice. Besides being characterized by a full use of small group discussions, as the primary means for stimulating thought, a leadership course had to provide its students with the opportunity of relating theory to practice in a variety of interesting and vivid ways. This could be done by incorporating practical observation exercises, films, and written case studies. In other words, the integrated and visual model of the three circles (see page 10) had to be clothed in flesh-and-blood by the practice and observation of students themselves, for one cannot teach leadership—it can only be learnt. The educational philosophy and methods of instruction needed to be as carefully thought out as the nature of leadership itself; only then could the marriage between thought and action prove to be a fruitful union.

One other largely fortuitous characteristic of Sandhurst leadership training is worth noting. The actual tutors or instructors on the concentrated two-day courses were all company commanders, the equivalents to line managers in industry. Moreover, on each occasion there would be twelve courses involving over 300 officer cadets running concurrently. Therefore the theoretical concepts had to be kept simple and the methods such that no special qualification in social psychology or expensive expertise was required in the teacher. After some 10 000 officer cadets in the British armed forces had completed the course (before 1968), it was established beyond all doubt that good results could be obtained by this combination of a very carefully designed course based on research and specialist training experience on the one hand, and the ability of Army, Royal Air Force, and Royal Navy officers on the other hand, in the midst of many other pressing duties, to get the hang of the course, and to improve their own performance as trainers 'on the job' with only a limited amount of explicit preparation for their role. As Adviser on Leadership Training at Sandhurst between 1963 and 1968, it was my responsibility to see that the results of the course did not fall below a certain standard; in fact, the natural ability and enthusiasm of many instructors frequently enabled them to achieve results well above that minimum level.

The interest of senior managers in industry led to the Sandhurst course being adapted and used for a series of one- or two-day seminars held in two United Kingdom firms—Wates Ltd, and Dorothy Perkins Ltd. Based on these results and independent inquiries, The Industrial Society, a self-financing body which places the development of leadership in industry among its five key aims, decided to adopt the functional approach towards the end of 1967. In the following year it arranged a number of seminars on this form of training for senior managers, and as a result the range of companies desiring to use this form of training increased. In October 1969 I accepted an invitation to join the Society for one year in order to establish a small leadership department so that

ACL training should be made much more widely available. By the end of 1970 over 5000 managers and supervisors had already attended ACL in-company courses led by training managers who had been on the Society's one- or two-day 'Training for Action-Centred Leadership' (TACL) courses.

Thus this book can be read partly as an interim report on progress so far in what is still a very young form of leadership development. Its rapid and solid growth is perhaps a testimony that it is filling a gap in management education of which more and more organizations have become aware. Certainly ACL is not a panacea, a cure-all or a substitute for high standards in other aspects of the practice of management. Yet if both ACL theory and methods are thoroughly understood and interpreted imaginatively in terms of a particular organizational setting, this kind of leadership training has a valuable contribution to make to management development, as the contributors to this book bear ample witness.

Neither this book nor the developments it narrates could have been possible without the help of many people. My debts to the staff at Sandhurst and to other individuals closely connected with the early evolution of ACL training, I have acknowledged elsewhere. Here I should like to express my warmest thanks, first, to John Garnett, CBE, the Director, the Advisers, and the administrative staff of The Industrial Society. The members of the Leadership Department, since its inception in 1969, have been, in chronological order of joining : Douglas Morgan, David Charles-Edwards, Frederick Patten (subsequently Head of Department), Elizabeth Andrews, Michael Bailey, Roger Felgate, Alan Ivens, Geoffrey Pope and Chris Sykes. Nigel Nicholls and Cliff Handscomb have made substantial contributions as associate advisers. Mary Vivian, Rosemary Hall and Faye Holtmon have been the admirable Administrative Officers.

My second major debt of gratitude, of course, is to those who have responded so readily to my invitation to write contributions or background papers for this book. Quite apart from the intrinsic value of their contributions, the willingness of these busy people to share their experience of ACL with others is surely a noteworthy fact. Certainly I am immensely grateful to them, and to those many other training managers and officers whom I have had the good fortune to meet and work with in the past five years. Those who have written pieces especially for this book kindly agreed to let me edit or use as background material their contributions according to the overall design. Thus some have been printed almost in full, and some only in brief extract or quotation. But I am deeply thankful for all the papers, and consequently I have found my editorial task to be an unenviable one. The experience and honest comments of actual practitioners are essential if management training is to make progress, and so I trust the reader will share my appreciation for the following twenty-six contributors:

Wing Commander Arthur Adamson, MBE (Royal Air Force).
Edwin P. Smith (The Industrial Society).
Ray Shaw (Fisons Ltd).
F. J. Peacock (National Westminster Bank Ltd).
W. J. Owens (South-East Metropolitan Hospital Area).
H. Lomas, CBE (Chief Officer, City of Manchester Fire Brigade).
Edwin Hutchinson (National Coal Board).
K. S. Connor (Postal Business Supervisory Training Centre).
Frederick Patten (The Industrial Society).
F. H. Trenchard (The British Oxygen Company Ltd).
J. S. W. Lyons & J. Frost (Caterpillar Tractor Company Ltd).
John Fry (Abbey National Building Society).
Michael Amies (Kalamazoo Ltd).
A. H. Extance (Reed International Ltd).
C. J. Hayes (Vauxhall Motors Ltd).
D. Tamblin (London Borough of Hillingdon).
T. R. Johnson (British Insulated Callender's Cables Ltd).
Geoffrey Halden (W. H. Smith Ltd).
Michael Bailey (The Industrial Society).
David Shepherd (Cadbury Schweppes Ltd).
John Young (Hoover Ltd).
Mrs M. Pearson (John Lewis Partnership).
G. A. G. Ormsby (The Administrative Staff College).
Richard Matanle (Oxfam).
Nigel Nicholls (Associate Adviser, The Industrial Society).

1. The nature of leadership

The nature of leadership

In this chapter I shall outline a general concept of leadership and some educational principles relevant to it: taken together they are the twin pillars upon which the practical leadership training described in following chapters rests. Therefore no apology is required for this excursion into the academic study of leadership, for training which is not based on sound and tested concepts eventually withers like a plant starved by weak roots; it may blossom for a day, but it cannot withstand the buffets of adverse winds. Nor does the possession of a firm conceptual framework mean that the trainer must be able to invoke a yard-long pedigree of experimental research papers printed in obscure psychological journals. My contention is rather that the roots of training must tap a living stream of truth about man, which flows and filters underground and is known only by its refreshing powers and the fruits which it produces.

The best academic research seeks to chart and sample this water. In the following sections I shall plot the main lines of inquiry and research into the nature of leadership, from which emerges what I hope is an intellectually satisfying and practically useful concept of leadership.

QUALITIES APPROACH

The traditional approach to defining leadership has been the age-old attempt to list the traits of a leader, such as courage, honesty, judgement, and humour. In *Training for Leadership*, by publishing the lists of traits taught or recommended in the Western world at officer training schools, I showed that there was little or no agreement on what these qualities might be in the military field. Nor have studies of management and supervisory leadership, which claimed to be objective, established any common list of necessary personal qualities.[1]

3

For example, a study by Professor C. Bird of the University of Minnesota in 1940 looked at 20 experimental investigations into leadership and found that only 5 per cent of the traits appear in four or more of the lists.[2] After a comprehensive survey of 124 books and articles which reported attempts to study the traits and characteristics of leaders, R. M. Stogdill offered two conclusions based on positive evidence from 15 or more of the studies surveyed :

- The average person who occupies a position of leadership exceeds the average member of his group in the following respects: (a) intelligence, (b) scholarship, (c) dependability in exercising responsibilities, (d) activity and social participation, and (e) socio-economic status.
- The qualities, characteristics, and skills required in a leader are determined to a large extent by the demands of the situation in which he is to function as a leader.

Moreover, despite considerable evidence to the contrary, 'the general trend of results suggests a low positive correlation between leadership and such variables as chronological age, height, weight, physique, energy, appearance, dominance, and mood control. The evidence is about evenly divided concerning the relation to leadership of such traits as introversion-extroversion, self-sufficiency, and emotional control.'[3] C. A. Gibb summed up the message of this and other studies : 'A leader is not a person characterized by any particular and consistent set of personality traits.'[4]

We should, however, be cautious of deducing from this negative finding the false conclusion that the personality and character of the leader do not matter. Stogdill merely recorded the conclusions of many students that the personality and character traits which were important depended upon the given group and situation, and that they could not be identified in a universal sense. Secondly, his article revealed some of the methodological inadequacies of research into personality traits : for example, he only looked at those factors which were studied by three or more investigators. It may be that the concepts and the methods used by researchers before 1948 (or since) were just not accurate enough to capture and measure the mysterious essence of leadership.

Certainly we do know a little about the qualities of leadership. There is general agreement, for example, that leaders should reflect or personify the qualities expected or required in their groups or organizations. It is quite possible, too, that further research will also demonstrate the universal presence of certain characteristics (received as gifts from heredity and environment but fashioned or actualized in the stream of experience) in

4

effective or successful leaders, such as a sense of responsibility, moral courage, judgement, and integrity. These characteristics are notoriously difficult to define or study in comparison with, for example, intelligence. Moreover, the notions of effectiveness and success demand definitions which cannot avoid value judgements. Therefore, like the hard questions in an examination paper, the research students have continually deferred them to some future date.[5]

While recognizing the valuable contribution which the traits approach to leadership has already made, and the opportunities it still affords for further research, we may conclude that taken by itself it is inadequate as the sole theoretical component of leadership training programmes. 'Smith is not a born leader yet,' wrote one senior manager on a junior's report. What can either Smith or his boss do about it? Not much, at least in the short term. The quotation aptly captures the dilemma of those who put all their eggs into the traits theoretical basket; logically the approach favours selection rather than training. This does not mean that an individual's attempts to develop his own character are necessarily without value or fruit; it merely implies that such endeavours take a long time and that they cannot be organized or relied upon by others in contemporary society. Certainly the attitudes engendered in both teachers and learners when the traits approach is held as an unexamined and largely unconscious assumption, buttressed by miscellaneous prejudices, are not conducive to significant discovery, development and growth through training programmes.

SITUATIONAL APPROACH

A year before R. M. Stogdill's article, W. O. Jenkins published his summary of 72 books and articles on military leadership. He concluded that :

'Leadership is specific to the particular situation under investigation. Who becomes a leader of a particular group engaging in a particular activity and what the characteristics are in the given case are a function of the specific situation. . . .'[6]

As already noted Stogdill endorsed this conclusion, which emphasized the technical or general competence of the leader in terms of the given situation—the *Admirable Crichton* theory. The situational approach possesses a self-evident importance, for we can all think of leaders who are highly adapted to one kind of group or situation, and who could not be visualized as leading in a different set of circumstances. There is a

5

real sense in which 'authority flows from the man who knows'. Yet technical knowledge and skill by themselves are certainly not guarantees of leadership, as some ardent situationalists have affirmed. The traits or qualities approach had indeed tried to define the wider requirements for leadership, those which could not be related solely to competence in a given situation, but with little success.

One logical development of this situational theory has been to suggest that two different leaders are required in each group : one for 'instrumental' work towards the goal and one for the 'socio-emotional' role general to all situations.

Professor F. E. Fiedler of the University of Illinois and his associates investigated the extent to which leadership veered towards the two poles of 'task oriented' and 'considerate' (or 'human relations') and tried to predict the circumstances in which one of these leadership 'styles' would be more effective than the other. Their work bears some resemblance to the well-known Grid method of management training devised by R. Blake and J. Mouton, which sought to develop an awareness in managers of the 'style' to which their personality veered, by assigning numbers to the various possibilities. Fiedler also seems to suggest that it might be less trouble to change the situation than to train the leader : 'Up to now we may have paid too much attention to selecting and training leaders and too little to the situation. It is obviously easier to change someone's rank and power, or to modify the job he is supposed to do, than it is to change his personality or leadership style. We can improve the effectiveness of leadership by accurate diagnosis of the group-task situation and by altering the leader's work environment.'[7]

It is doubtful, however, whether altering group composition, the task structure and 'position power' to suit a leader's bias would prove to be a less demanding proposition than developing the leadership potential in those leaders carefully selected for the general work environment, so that they could respond to the needs of the situation. With such training the leaders concerned could learn to change the situations themselves, and not wait for someone else to change them for them. And they would do this not in order to be personally more adapted, but so that a shared progress can be achieved towards common goals.

GROUP APPROACH

In close connection with the situational approach and stemming from the observation of small groups in the 'Group Laboratories' of the early group dynamics movement at Bethel in the United States, the notion became widely accepted that leadership could be regarded as a disembodied process which could be shared by some or all members of the group. Whoever happened to be providing a needed or effective function at a given time was the leader for the moment. An appointed or designated leader was only necessary as a safety net if the group failed to direct itself. The distinction between leader and follower was blurred in every possible way. As late as 1969, C. A. Gibb could write :

> 'The study of leadership is essentially one aspect of the study of the mechanisms devised by groups for the efficient pursuit of their goals and for the satisfaction by members of those needs which have been group-invested. By a mechanism of role differentiation, groups use the differential characteristics of members to the advantage of all by assigning group tasks to those best qualified to perform them. Leadership is an aspect of this process. . . . It is to groups rather than to individuals that the concept of leadership is applicable.'[8]

The contribution of social psychology to our knowledge of leadership has undoubtedly been great, but the drawbacks of the group approach as a complete explanation of the phenomena of leadership have become increasingly manifest. The present author listed and discussed some major criticisms of the approach in 1968.[9] In particular the group theorists had failed to apply their theory to themselves, in the sense that they had not realized that their views of reality were shaped by the highly artificial situation of the group dynamics laboratory and the 'T-Group' training session. In particular, the absence of any real task from the group dynamics groups mitigated against the chances that concepts of leadership formed from them would be applicable to more realistic situations. Douglas McGregor graphically pointed out (after becoming a college president) that in his earlier teaching days, under the influence of 'human relations' theory, he had seriously underwritten the responsibilities and burdens of good leadership.[10]

Moreover, it has become increasingly clear that value judgements drawn from a given culture in general and the philosophical assumptions of university behavioural scientists in the 1950s and 1960s in particular coloured the conclusions which were drawn. Group leadership looked on the surface more 'democratic' than the older traditional traits view, which seemed to justify what was deemed to be 'authoritarian' or 'autocratic' leadership. Various strands, such as Freudian psychology and the post-war rejection of anything smacking of the *fuehrer-prinzep*,

7

mingled with these political and cultural preconceptions to elevate the group and lower the leader. The group school saw the latter as simply a group member who differed from his fellow group members only in the quantity of the acts of influence he contributed, but not in any quality.

Through the great boom in management education in the 1960s these doctrines about leadership, despite the scepticism of experienced managers, scholars, and leaders, entered into the orthodoxies expounded in the training institutes, business schools, and courses to a whole generation. For one reason or another the critical comments or warning notes of such men as William Whyte, Douglas McGregor, and Lydall Urwick were ignored or dismissed by the group dynamics school.[11] In some cases they even identified group dynamics 'T-Group' training with leadership training. Gradually, however, the importation of alien values and assumptions into what has purported to be behavioural science has been more and more widely noted. In 1965, for example, the widely respected Professor A. H. Maslow commented in his observations on a group dynamics laboratory :

'What I smell here is again some of the democratic dogma and piety in which all people are equal and in which the conception of a factually strong person or natural leader or dominant person or superior intellect or superior decisiveness or whatever is bypassed because it makes everybody uncomfortable and because it seems to contradict the democratic philosophy (of course, it does *not* really contradict it).'[12]

THE THREE-CIRCLES MODEL

Several writers have attempted to produce a synthetic portrait of leadership by simply relating the three main approaches outlined above to each other. But something more has to be added to the picture if their positive contributions are to be seen to the best advantage. In this section a model of groups or organizations is presented which not only has served to integrate for many people the research findings so far gleaned but also has proved in itself to be an acceptable basis for leadership training and development programmes.

As a starting point I have developed the idea that working groups resemble individuals in that although they are always unique (each develops its own 'group personality') yet they share, as do individuals, certain common 'needs'. There are three areas of need present in such groups. Two of these are the properties of the group as a whole, namely *the need to accomplish the common task* and *the need to be maintained as a cohesive social unity* (which I have called the 'team maintenance need'). The third area is constituted by the sum of the *individual needs* of group members.[13]

With regard to the third area, it may be noted in parenthesis, that experienced leaders in all periods of history have realized that man lives by more than bread alone. Only comparatively recently, however, has the work of psychologists thrown clearer light on the nature of the needs which individuals take with them wherever they go, by virtue of being human. Professor A. H. Maslow categorized these needs into the well-known following hierarchy: physiological (e.g. food, water); safety (e.g. security); social (e.g. acceptance, belongingness); esteem (e.g. self-respect, recognition, status); and self-actualization (i.e. realization of one's latent potential).[14] Professor Frederick Herzberg has dichotomized the list by suggesting that the factors which make people experience satisfaction in their work situation are not the reverse of those which make them dissatisfied. The latter is caused by deficiencies in the environment or context of the job; in contrast, job satisfaction rests upon the content of the work and the opportunities it presents for achievment, recognition, professional development, and personal growth.[15]

The first major point is that these three areas of need influence each other for better or worse. For example, if a group fails in its task this will intensify the disintegrative tendencies present in the group and raise a diminished satisfaction for its individual members. If there is a lack of unity or harmonious relationships in the group this will affect performance on the job and also individual needs (cf. A. H. Maslow's Social Needs). And obviously an individual who feels frustrated and unhappy in a particular work environment will not make his maximum contribution to either the common task or to the life of the group.

Conversely, achievement in terms of a common aim tends to build a sense of group identity—the 'we-feeling', as some have called it. The moment of victory closes the psychological gaps between people: morale rises naturally. Good internal communications and a developed team spirit based upon past successes makes a group much more likely to do well in its task area, and incidentally provides a more satisfactory climate for the individual. Lastly, an individual whose needs are recognized and who feels that he can make a characteristic and worthwhile contribution both to the task and the group will tend to produce good fruits in both these areas.

We can illustrate these interrelations with a simple model :

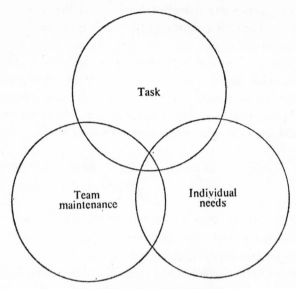

Fig 1.1. *Interaction of Needs*

In order for the needs in these areas to be met in any group or organization certain *functions* have to be performed. According to this integrated theory the provision of these necessary functions is the responsibility of leadership, although that does not imply that the leader will perform all of them himself. Indeed, in groups over the size of about five members there are too many functions required for any one person to supply them all himself.

Various attempts have been made to list the functions in recent years, but they suffer from several disadvantages. In the first place, some researchers have produced three separate lists, one for each area. The difference between 'task' and 'team maintenance' is always in danger of yawning into a dichotomy. The value of the three *overlapping* circles is that they emphasize the essential unity of leadership : a single action can be multi-functional in that it touches all three areas. The distinction between the circles should not therefore be pressed too far, and separate lists favour that unfortunate tendency. Secondly, many of the lists reflect the group dynamics laboratory situation too much. Thirdly, it is rather artificial to categorize the response of leaders to individual needs. It is sufficient to recognize that effective leaders are aware of this dimen-

10

sion, and respond in appropriate ways with understanding. Such action might range from changing the content of an individual's job or role, along the lines advocated by Professor Herzberg, to a promotion or a word of encouragement.

It is perhaps best to work out a single list of leadership functions within the context of a given working situation, so that the sub-headings can have the stamp of reality upon them. But there is general agreement upon the essentials, and to illustrate some of these major functions meeting the three interacting areas of need, I give here a list originally worked out at the Royal Military Academy, Sandhurst, which has been the basis for numerous adaptations in industry and other fields :

- Planning : e.g. Seeking all available information.
  Defining group task, purpose or goal.
  Making a workable plan (in right decision-making framework).

- Initiating : e.g. Briefing group on the aims and the plan.
  Explaining why aim or plan is necessary.
  Allocating tasks to group members.
  Setting group standards.

- Controlling : e.g. Maintaining group standards.
  Influencing tempo.
  Ensuring all actions are taken towards objectives.
  Keeping discussion relevant.
  Prodding group to action/decision.

- Supporting : e.g. Expressing acceptance of persons and their contribution.
  Encouraging group/individuals.
  Disciplining group/individuals.
  Creating team spirit.
  Relieving tension with humour.
  Reconciling disagreements or getting others to explore them.

- Informing : e.g. Clarifying task and plan.
  Giving new information to the group, i.e. keeping them 'in the picture'.
  Receiving information from group.
  Summarizing suggestions and ideas coherently.

- Evaluating : e.g. Checking feasibility of an idea.
  Testing the consequences of a proposed solution.

11

Evaluating group performance.

Helping the group to evaluate its own performance against standards.

My experience in the last few years has convinced me that the search for a verbal unanimity in the language of functions is as likely to be as unsuccessful as the quest for a common agreement on trait names. The word 'function' itself is open to different interpretations. Within limits some diversity is always to be welcomed. After all, the first aim in leadership training is to help people to think deeply for themselves, not to utter a final word intended to stop all further questions or developments. But the open or unfinished nature of our present lists of leadership functions makes it imperative that we retain the trefoil model as a reference point for discussions of what functions are required as well as a continual reminder of *why* they are needed.

It could be argued, as the group-centred theorists did, that these are *membership* functions, and that whoever happens to be performing one of them was the present leader. This view, however, rests upon an assumption which turns out to be a half-truth, namely that leadership exists to meet group needs. This group-centred concept cannot bear all the weight that has been placed upon it, for reality is far more complex. There are three main ways by which a person can become a leader : emergence, election, or appointment. Most leaders arrive by a combination of two or more of these methods. Where the task is *given* from outside or above to a group or organization, the leadership tends to be given (appointed) with it, so to speak; and these leaders are responsible outwards and upwards for getting the task achieved. This fact sets apart work groups in industry from those voluntary groups, such as sports or social clubs, which not only band together for some purpose or aim of their own choosing but also elect a leadership responsible only to them for its attainment. Now groups in laboratory situation, or in the training method originally known as group dynamics, belong generally more to the latter range of groups, and we can see why the problem of the transference of assumptions and concepts from that situation to the working environment of people deserved the greater attention that it is now receiving.

A British test pilot and former Squadron Leader, David Stinton, has expressed the extreme counter-view both strongly and provocatively :

'As far as the leader is concerned, he is not one of a group; and if he is a true leader and not just a bell-wether (the lead sheep in a

12

flock with a bell around its neck, that the rest will follow) he never will belong. A leader is always something of an outsider. He must see over the heads of the group and beyond it. He has more 'stature' in the sense that one can measure the stature of a man by how far he sees. Very often leaders see so far that they are not recognized early. They are prophets whom lesser men fail to understand. It is only when the coincidence of vision and moment is right that what the leader has to say makes sense to lesser men.'[16]

As so often is the case the truth lies somewhere in between the two extremes : in working groups the leader is in the group but not *of* it. As this book is primarily concerned with leadership in groups or organizations where the task is in some sense given and the leader appointed it seems right to ask how far the leader should share or delegate the necessary functions which are his responsibility with other members of the group, rather than how far the group should share its powers with him. We may recall that some degree of sharing is necessary in groups over a certain size : there is always plenty of opportunity for members to contribute towards team maintenance and the satisfaction of individual needs. In organizations we need a concept of the management (or the equivalent term) as the corporate leadership responsible together, like a body with different functions, for the provision of the necessary actions and influences in the three interlocking areas. The potential value of the model as a single integrating theory capable of bringing order into the present profusion of organizational theories will be discussed later.

Without forgetting the broader opportunities open to members for supplementing the work of leadership in all three areas described above it is especially useful to examine specifically the extent to which the leader should share with others the general function of *decision-making*, the core of such more definite functions as setting objectives and planning.

In an invaluable diagram R. Tannenbaum and W. H. Schmidt[17] plotted the possibilities of participation. The diagram can be compared to a cake : at one end the leader has virtually all of it, and at the other the group has the lion's share. In terms of a transaction between a leader and an individual follower the continuum also illustrates the degrees of delegation that are possible in the context of a given decision.

There is much to be said (and that has been said) for moving as far to the right of the continuum as possible, for the more that people share in decisions which directly affect them the more they are motivated to carry them out—providing they trust the integrity of the leader who is

13

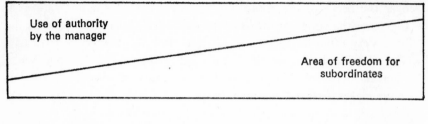

Use of authority
by the manager

Area of freedom for
subordinates

| Manager makes decision and announces it | Manager 'sells' decision | Manager presents ideas & invites questions | Manager presents tentative decision subject to change | Manager presents problem, gets suggestions, makes decision | Manager defines limits; asks group to make decision | Manager permits subordinates to function within limits defined by superior |

Fig 1.2. *A Continuum of Shared Decisions*

inviting them to participate in the decision. Yet factors in the *situation* (especially the nature of the task and the time available for the decision) and the *group* (especially the attitudes, knowledge, and experience of members) will naturally limit the extent to which the right-hand edge of the continuum can be approached. Other limiting factors may be present in the personality of the leader or the value system and philosophy of a particular organization, factors which cannot be described as natural or intrinsic in the same way as the situational or group constraints.

There are some groups and organizations whose *characteristic* working situation (as contrasted to the actual ones they may be in for 90 per cent of their time) are essentially crisis ones, where by definition time is short for decisions and the matter of life or death rests upon prompt decisions from one man e.g. operating theatre teams, fire brigades, police forces, air line crews, and military organizations. Yet such groups are not always in crisis situations, and for training purposes, if for no other reason, they need to explore the decision-making scale. Moreover, although it is not always possible to share decisions over *ends* (i.e. goals, objectives, aims or purpose) it is usually possible to involve others more or less fully in *means* (i.e. methods, techniques, conditions, and plans).

Rather than engaging in the fruitless attempt to establish a particular spot or 'style' on the scale which is 'best' we should see the continuum as a sliding scale, or as a thermometer marked with boiling and freezing points.[18] Where the latter points fall on the scale will depend upon the characteristic working situation of the group or organization. There will

14

be a difference, for example, between an earth-shifting gang of labourers constructing a motorway and a research group in an electronics or chemical firm.

CONCLUSION

We can now construct a general idea or integrated concept of a leader as a person with certain *qualities* of personality and character, which are appropriate to the general *situation* and supported by a degree of relevant technical knowledge and experience, who is able to provide the necessary *functions* to guide a group towards the further realization of its purpose, while maintaining and building its unity as a team; doing all this in the right ratio or proportion with the contributions of other members of the team. The length of this last sentence clearly precludes it from ever becoming a slick definition, but it is a framework for drawing together the major strands of research into the nature of leadership without exhausting the inherent mystery present in it as in all human relations.

REFERENCES AND COMMENTS

1. For a stimulating commentary on this point, see Vance Packard, *The Pyramid Climbers*, Penguin Books, (1965). Especially chapter 12, 'The Search for Ideal Types'.
2. C. Bird, *Social Psychology*, Appleton-Century, (1940), 378–379.
3. R. M. Stogdill, 'Personal Factors associated with Leadership: A Survey of the Literature', *Journal of Psychology*, **25**, (1948), 54–79. For an excellent summary of the inadequacies of this approach, see Alvin Gouldner (ed.) *Studies in Leadership*, Harper (1950), 23–45.
4. C. A. Gibb (ed.), *Leadership: Selected Readings*, Penguin Books, (1969), 11. This book contains a reprint of R. M. Stogdill's article.
5. *Cf.* 'Problems which appear to be in need of thorough investigation are those relating to factors which condition social participation, insight into situations, mood control, responsibility, and transferability of leadership from one situation to another. Answers to these questions seem basic not only to any adequate understanding of the personal qualifications of leaders, but also to any effective training for leadership.' R. M. Stogdill, *op. cit.*, 79.
6. W. O. Jenkins, 'A Review of Leadership Studies with particular reference to Military Problems,' *Psychological Bulletin*, **44**, (1947), 54–79.
7. F. E. Fiedler, 'Leadership—A new model', *Discovery*, (April 1965) and, *A Theory of Leadership effectiveness*, McGraw-Hill, (1967). For an appraisal, see W. Hill, 'An Empirical Test of Fiedler's Contingency Model of Leadership Effectiveness in Three Organizations', *The Southern Journal of Business*, (July 1969). See also, R. Blake and J. Mouton, *The Management Grid*, Houston, Gulf Publishing, (1964). For further examples of the situationalist approach, see Bavelas, 'Leadership: Man and Function', *Administrative Science Quarterly*, **5**, (1960), 491–498, and Bales and Slater, 'Role Differentiation in Small Decision-Making Groups', in Talcott Parsons, *et al.*, *Family, Socialization and Interaction Process*, Glencoe: Free Press, (1955). For the origins of the 'styles' preoccupation (in the work of Kurt Lewin), see Lewin and Lippitt, 'An Experi-

15

mental Approach to the Study of Autocracy and Democracy: A Preliminary Note', *Sociometry*, **1**, (1938), 292–300.

8. *Leadership: Selected Readings, op. cit.*, 10.

9. J. Adair, *Training for Leadership*, Macdonald (1968), 119–127.

10. *Leadership and Motivation, Essays of Douglas McGregor*, W. G. Bennis and E. H. Schein (eds.), The M.I.T. Press, (1966); quoted in J. Adair, *op. cit.*, 122–123.

11. William H. Whyte, Jr., *The Organization Man*, Simone and Schuster, (1955); L. F. Urwick, 'Management in Human Relations', in R. Tannenbaum, I. R. Weschler, F. Massarik, *Leadership and Organization: A Behavioural Science Approach*, McGraw-Hill, (1961).

12. A. H. Maslow, *Eupsychian Management: A Journal*, Richard D. Irwin, (1965).

13. For the consensus of evidence concerning the existence of such clearly discernible areas, and the different responses they require, see C. A. Gibb (ed.), *op. cit.*, 13 and elsewhere.

14. A. H. Maslow, *Motivation and Personality*, Harper, (1954).

15. F. Herzberg, *Work and the Nature of Man*, World Publishing Co., (1966).

16. *Air Clues* (Royal Air Force journal), November 1968.

17. R. Tannenbaum and W. H. Schmidt, 'How to Choose a Leadership Pattern', *Harvard Business Review*, March–April (1958).

18. For confirmation of this point in particular, and for a discussion of sharing decisions in general, see F. A. Heller, *Managerial Decision-making: A Study of Leadership Styles and Power Sharing*, Tavistock Publications, (1971).

2. The ACL course

INTRODUCTION (BY JOHN ADAIR)

Many books on management training fail to give the reader a clear idea of the methods in question, or what actually happens during the training. To ensure that this book provides this basic information, Edwin Smith describes in some detail the industrial application of the one and a half day course first developed in the Armed Services. Much of the remainder of this book deals with further applications, developments, and evaluations of this basic framework, and so this chapter will provide a necessary foundation.

In 1969, Edwin Smith wrote The Action-Centred Leader Course Tutor's Manual, *which most ably translated the original course from its military setting into a form which could be understood and used by industrial training managers in Britain and overseas. Within two years of its publication, over 300 firms and organizations in Britain proved the value of the manual by using it in their in-company training programmes.*

After nearly 30 years of practical experience in the chemical and food industries as research chemist, production chemist, and manager of control and development, Edwin Smith took a degree in business management. He joined The Industrial Society management advisory staff in 1967, specializing in Management by Objectives and Leadership Development. He is also author of the highly successful short booklet: The Manager as an Action-Centred Leader.

The ACL course

Edwin P. Smith

THE ACL COURSE

To some managers, whether in commerce, public service, or industry, the relevance of leadership to management is not immediately apparent. It may help to an understanding of the connection if we define that part of a manager's job concerned with getting the best contribution from those for whose work he is responsible as—*leadership*.

In the case of a 'leadered' group, such as inevitably exists in business, that which characterizes the leader is by no means confined to his personality, his presence, his 'charisma'. What *actions* the leader performs *and how he performs them* is also a vital factor in the formula which represents the successful manager.

It is these actions, these functions of the leader, which are capable of being learned and developed to improve a manager's performance in maximizing his human resource. Both the awareness and the skills which combine to produce this ability can be developed and, from time to time, need to be refreshed. The Action-Centred Leadership course concentrates on the actions and awareness necessary to improve leadership performance.

The Aims of the Course
To be efficient a manager needs :

- technical competence sufficient to manage the technology of the job
- sufficient knowledge to cover the 'technical' aspects of management
- ability to get the best work out of those for whose work he is responsible and accountable.

It can, and does, happen that a manager has a more than sufficient competence in the requisite technology and also in the techniques of management, yet, at the same time, is ineffective in the use of the human resources; that is, he is a poor leader.

This course arises directly from the urgent need to develop in those capable of benefiting—the potential leaders and many existing managers, untrained in leadership—their ability to lead.

More specifically, the course is designed to improve a manager's leadership back on the job :

- By awakening APPRECIATION of the the essential FUNCTIONS of the leader.
- By developing RECOGNITION of the FUNCTIONS of the leader—when observing them in practice.
- By testing, in the case of a few members of the course, their ability to APPLY the new knowledge of the FUNCTIONS of the leader. For the rest, to encourage this APPLICATION on their return to the work situation.

The Course Method. The emphasis of the course is on observing and participating in practical exercises. Formal lectures are kept to the absolute minimum and every member of the course takes part in exercises, group discussion, and case studies.

Because of the importance of individual involvement the maximum number of course members should be 24, although a smaller group of not less than 10 is viable (five for an exercise and five to observe). It has been found that a minimum amount of pre-course work saves valuable programme time.

Tutor's Role. The tutor's role is two-fold :

- To promote understanding of :
  (*a*) the concept of functional leadership,
  (*b*) the practical implications of functional leadership within the members' own practical situation.
- To ensure that :
  (*a*) everyone participates and that tasks are fairly distributed,
  (*b*) the lessons learnt at each session are relevant to the stated purpose of the session and that vital ones are not overlooked by stating the aim of each session at the start, and finally checking how well this has been achieved.

20

Leadership exercises. Vital to the success of this course are the leadership exercises. The purpose of these practical exercises is to give an individual member practice in leading, at the same time giving the rest of the team participating roles in a leadership situation and the rest of the course the opportunity to observe the leaders' actions or omissions and to learn from his successes and failures. The leader is given as free a role as possible without allowing the exercise to deteriorate into collapse through bad leadership. Lessons can be learnt from the latter situation, but the experience is liable to be too traumatic to be practical in the training situation.

Since a manager is almost invariably a leader appointed by higher management and not elected by his subordinates, the course exercises are not designed for 'leaderless' groups, where the leader naturally emerges from the group. For each exercise, therefore, the leader should be chosen by the course tutor who, either explicitly, or implicitly, thereby invests him with sufficient authority to achieve the given task.

A crucial part of the leadership exercises is the assessment by both the team and the observers of the leadership during the operation. To aid recollection this is conducted immediately the exercise is finished, by which time the observers are required to have completed a Leadership Observation Sheet on which is recorded actual events, comments, and reactions as they occurred. The data must be factual—'He did (not) tell the team what exactly they were supposed to be doing' is acceptable. 'He communicated well' or 'he was a powerful leader' is not.

The observers are looking for actual signs (or their absence) of leadership within the operation of the three areas—achieving the task, keeping group cohesion, and satisfying individual needs.

The tutor is not only responsible for seeing that the performance of the team leader is assessed accurately but also for ensuring that each observer has shown by the data he has produced that he is capable of recognizing leadership functions in action. This he does by asking specific questions of the observers, insisting on evidence to back up their answers. Finally he summarizes the lessons to be learned from the exercise and will continue to do this throughout the course. Thus the involvement of all those taking part is an essential feature of the course.

Course Programme
The typical programme of a two-day course shows that the twelve sessions include periods involving tutor explanation, group discussion, group reporting, and several types of exercise.

Continuing the practical nature of the course and the stated objective to improve each manager's leadership back on the job the final session is one of personal commitment in which each delegate is encouraged to

TABLE 2.1. A Specimen Course Programme

SESSION	DAY 1	SESSION	DAY 2
1	9.30 INTRODUCTION Course objective Definition of need for leadership 9.55 GROUP DISCUSSION 10.30 REPORT BACK—Discuss 10.45 THE QUALITIES, SITUATIONAL & FUNCTIONAL APPROACH TO LEADERSHIP	7	9.45—PART II 10.45 ANALYSIS & DISCUSSION Practice in identifying & observing leadership
2	11.15 LEADERSHIP EXERCISE I *12.00 OBSERVATIONS & DISCUSSION Practice in observing Leadership	8	11.30 LEADERSHIP EXERCISE III ANALYSIS & DISCUSSION Further practice in observing leadership
3	12.15 SHARING DECISIONS 12.45 (approx) Lunch	9	12.15 PRACTICAL IMPLICATIONS OF THE MODEL 12.45 (approx) Lunch
4	2.00 LEADERSHIP EXERCISE II OBSERVATION & DISCUSSION	10	2.00 AN ORGANIZATIONAL STUDY Practical implications applied
5	2.45 MOTIVATION	11	REPORTING BACK ON ORGANIZATIONAL CASE STUDY
6	3.30 LEADERSHIP FILM— PART I ANALYSIS & DISCUSSION Practice in identifying and observing leadership	12	3.45 DISCUSSION OF GROUP REPORTING BACK ACTION FOLLOWING THE COURSE 4.45 Course Conclusion

* Exact timing to depend on exercise selected

state the actions he intends to take back in the work situation resulting from the course.

Delegates are given handouts throughout the course to aid recollection of the principles and the functions of leadership covered. Each session starts with an explanation of its stated aim and ends with a summary of the items relevant to leadership which have been discovered. A more detailed explanation of the course, session by session, follows.

Session One. This starts with the tutor explaining the aims of the course (q.v.). He then explains the need for the manager in business, industry, or commerce to be a good leader, since he is required to encourage the best performance from those for whose work he is responsible. Evidence is briefly adduced supporting the principle that this type of leadership is a function not solely of the personality of the manager, nor of the situation or the climate in which he operates but also of the actions he takes in achieving his objectives successfully. The awareness of the need for leadership training is thus aroused in the members of the course.

The course is then divided into groups of not more than eight and each instructed to discuss and report back their answers to some such questions as—'What should a leader BE to lead effectively?' and 'What should a leader DO to lead effectively?' The purpose of this exercise is to get delegates, early in the course, digging for answers out of their own experience. This enables them the easier to identify with the purpose of the course.

The findings of the groups are analysed in plenary session which then leads directly into an explanation of the three approaches to leadership covered in the first chapter—the qualities, situational, and functional approaches.

Session Two. Through a practical exercise course members are given practice in the observation of leadership functions. A team of five is chosen from the course members and one of their number appointed leader. He is briefed out of earshot of the rest of the team but in the presence of the rest of the course who are observing. The observers are then briefed on the use of the Observation Sheet.

The exercise now starts and is allowed to proceed for the allotted time. The leader and team are then thanked for performing the task thus providing the opportunity for others to observe and for the tutor to test the observers' ability to recognize leadership in action. This testing of the ability of observers to recognize the leadership functions is a crucial part of all the exercises. It provides the opportunity for all to learn and is vital to the success of the course.

Going through the relevant functions the tutor requires the observers to produce evidence and to 'speak to data'.

'Was the task achieved?' 'If not, why not?'
'Which of the functions should have applied here?'
'Which were done? How well? Which omitted?'
'Were the needs of each of the three areas served adequately?'
'Were the needs of one area allowed to dominate to the detriment of the task?'

Members of the participating team are asked whether they felt they were taking part as a team, or group or whether individuals were allowed to dominate.

The leader is asked to comment on his leadership in the light of the comments and his own analysis. 'What have you learned from the experience?' 'Repeating the exercise, what would you do differently, and why?' The tutor then summarizes the lessons learned, drawing attention especially to those functions which were omitted or performed inadequately thus affecting the result adversely. The kind of analysis here described is performed after each exercise during the course.

The actual exercise used varies according to the background of the course members but at this stage only an uncomplicated one is required. Those proving successful have involved the piecing together of two different jig-saw puzzles whose pieces have been mixed; the reassembling of two copies of different issues of a magazine previously reduced to their separate sheets and reassembled as a pile of completely haphazard sheets; the transporting of a team over a marked area on the floor (a pirhana-infested river) via planks and oil drums (or their equivalent in plastic shapes). A leader is appointed by the tutor for all these exercises and all are set to a time limit.

Session Three. By means of a dialogue with course members the tutor elicits that the categorizing of leadership styles into autocratic, bureaucratic, charismatic, democratic, and *laisser-faire* is inadequate since many variables are concerned.

Leadership style will be affected by such factors as the type of *organization* (its traditions and attitudes to authority); the *situation* (does the time available allow consultation in depth?); the expectation of *subordinates* (does their background, history, degree of education demand their greater involvement?); the *personality* of the leader himself (is it 'natural' for him to expect instant obedience to his orders or does he believe that in order to get the best out of people they must be involved

24

and consulted as much as possible?). The concept of the decision continuum (see p. 14) is then introduced and discussed.

In summary, the tutor emphasizes the point that in today's climate it is vital that whatever his natural leadership style the successful leader is one who has learned to be flexible and to suit his actions to the requirements of the often changing occasion.

Session Four. Through another exercise, this time more difficult, course members are given further practice in the observation of leadership functions and their awareness and skills as observers further developed.

An exercise calculated to give the right complexity at this stage of the course is one where the leader with a group of four others has, in twenty minutes, to produce a winning idea capable of persuading a rich Trust to award him £20 000 to be used for character training, educational, or social activities with young men of all levels under the age of twenty years. Unknown to the leader the individual members of his team are given roles to play. The leader is the personnel manager and his team is composed of the planning manager, a senior works foreman, the production manager and a trade union representative. The aspirations of each are different and there is here inherently a conflict situation to which the leader must find an answer. The usual assessment is made at the end of the exercise, the observers having noted their evidence (on their observation sheets) of leadership functions during it.

In summary, the tutor brings out the essential need of the leader to recognize the differing individual needs of his team and that unless the conflict is resolved successful achievement of the project is in jeopardy. At worst, the situation deteriorates and either the leader fails, or he uses autocratic power or a compromise is reached which does not satisfy all individual needs and group cohesion is lost. If a solution can be found which unites or integrates the differing needs, individuals can adapt to it, group unity is maintained and the task is successfully achieved. With the aid of a Leadership Checklist he analyses five functions of leadership in terms of action within each area of need.

Session Five. The purpose of this short session is to enable each delegate to understand the nature and individual needs of man at work and to know how to provide maximum opportunity for challenge, achievement and satisfaction within the work situation. By examining human behaviour more closely insights into motivation are widened and deepened.

25

The tutor briefly explains the work and the thinking of such people as McGregor (theory X and theory Y), Maslow (the hierarchy of needs) and Herzberg (hygiene-motivator theory), all concerned with a deeper understanding of the reasons why man works and his expectations from his life at work. A simple exercise (which could be pre-course work) concerned with ranking various motivational factors for both themselves and a subordinate enables course members to come more quickly to an understanding of those matters which influence the actions of man, both within and without the work situation.

After insights have been awakened or deepened the course then considers the practical implications for the leader in terms of what he needs to do if he is (as far as is practicable) to satisfy the needs of the individual members of his group. Recent examples are studied of how the jobs of a wide variety of people have been 'enriched' to the benefit both of the individual and the organization for which they were working.

Although one of the shortest sessions of the course this one is often one of the most rewarding for course members. In such cases a sudden enlightenment arises from the realization that feelings and conceptions they have vaguely felt, perhaps never expressed, have been shared by others and by some, actually translated into practical terms to the advantage of the individual, the group, the job, and the organization.

Sessions Six and Seven. The change of medium to a film gives course members further practice in the observation of contrasting types of leadership and in identifying the actions which it is necessary to take in particular leadership situations.

The most successful film from the point of view of giving course members further practice in identifying leadership actions has been a commercial, box-office success *Twelve O'Clock High* concerning the US Air Force flying the famous Flying Fortresses. Although the film pertains to a crisis situation in wartime, it is replete with examples of leadership actions in all three areas—task needs, group needs, and individual needs, and the great majority of managers are easily able to extrapolate from the crisis to the normal business, non-crisis situation.

During the first part of the film the leader of a bomb-group fails, is relieved of his post and another leader appointed. The film is stopped at this stage and the reasons for the failure of the first leader analysed. During the film the course members are making brief notes on observation sheets so that during the analysis they are required to give evidence for their assessments.

26

From answers to the question 'Why did the colonel fail?' the tutor elicits that 'he over-identified with the men'; he paid too much attention to individual needs at the expense of achieving the task and keeping the squadron together as a closely-knit group. The evidence in support of this thesis is collected, displayed, and analysed.

Before the second part of the film is shown the tutor gets from each individual course member an answer to his question 'What will this new leader do to recover the situation?' He gets each to judge whether the new leader will go first for task or team maintenance and asks for the grounds for such a decision. These decisions are then later compared against the actual ones as revealed in part two of the film and the implications of any discrepancies discussed.

After the second part is shown, from his question 'What has the new leader done?' the tutor elicits that he has concentrated on actions to satisfy team maintenance needs thereby successfully achieving the squadron's objectives. He further draws out that in doing so the leader improved discipline; set and maintained behaviour standards; insisted on training to raise standards; strengthened morale; achieved pride in the group; increased individual performance through getting identification and commitment and ensured the continued successful operation of the group after his departure or lapse from the group by ensuring continuity of leadership and succession.

Finally the actions or omissions of the two leaders are compared in their approaches to satisfying the individual needs of the main characters.

In summary, the tutor reiterates the lessons of a leader achieving his objectives through concentrating at various times on the task needs, the group needs, and the individual needs and also the necessity for a leader to decide on the priorities he must give to each area according to the situation. A leader must also have the skill and training to perform the functions to satisfy these needs.

Session Eight. Another practical group exercise enables one course member to practise leading four others and the rest of the course to observe leadership functions being performed.

A manager is responsible for producing certain results through providing and maximizing certain resources. He does not normally have resource to unlimited funds, countless personnel, or endless time. These, and others, are among the usual constraints within which he is obliged to operate.

This exercise is designed to test leadership in a situation in which these constraints operate. Within a specified time and with a given group and material provided, the leader must produce a tower built of small building bricks (e.g. Lego). His success will be measured in terms of financial profitability and this will be measured by computation from three profit or incentive graphs. In these graphs, profit is correlated with the height of the tower reached (performance); with the number of building bricks used (use of material); with time taken to build the tower (use of time). It is possible to make losses in all three areas; thus an overall loss.*

The exercise itself is divided into two phases—the planning phase (maximum 25 mins) and the construction phase (maximum 10 mins). During the planning phase the incentive graph should be studied and an optimum profit target selected. At the end of the planning phase the tutor is to be provided with the operating plan giving details of target profit, materials to be used, time to be taken, height to be attained, a rough sketch of the tower design, and a brief plan of construction. During the construction phase the tower is built by the team and the time taken noted. Throughout this exercise the tutor must be especially careful to see that the observers are concerned with observing the leader at work and not with the technical intricacies of the problem. At the conclusion of the exercise the relevant measurements are entered with the graphs, the overall profit or loss computed and the results displayed side by side with the stated targets.

For the majority of course members the main value of the exercise lies in the lessons learned during the leadership assessment session :

- Were the relevant skills within the group identified and used?
- When arriving at target plans were all the parameters taken into account?
- Was the group too eager to start experimenting with the building materials before a proper, viable plan had been made?
- Were one or two or more people virtually idle whilst the rest got involved in trial runs?
- Did the final results bear any relationship with the stated targets? If not, why not?
- Did the leader optimize his resources? Support your comments with evidence.

* This exercise—'The Mast Contract'—was freely adapted by the author of this chapter from an idea in an article entitled 'A Two-Hour Leadership Laboratory', in *The Training and Development Journal*, Vol. 22, No. 1, Jan. 1968.

Session Nine. The purpose of this session is to translate into practical terms for the manager the day-to-day implications of each of the three areas of need : task, group and individual.

Although we have seen leaders in action in short-time exercises, if functional leadership is to have any relevance at all it must also have meaning outside the training situation into every-day working life. With the exception of the one-man business, with which we are not concerned here, a manager, by definition, is one who works with and through others—a group. Such a working group differs from a crowd or random selection of individuals in that

- its members share a common aim, a purpose,
- its members must use their powers to keep the group as an operating unit and to protect it from those forces which threaten it, whilst supporting those forces which give it cohesion,
- the individual needs of its members must be satisfied in the long term.

It is the leader's job to see that all these three areas of need are met, in order persistently to achieve his objectives.

In his booklet *The Manager as an Action-Centred Leader* the writer has interpreted the functions which arise out of each area of need into specific actions the leader must take to get the job done well. These take the form of check lists which are now discussed, analysed, and illustrated in plenary session.

These check lists include, for instance :

(a) *Achieving the Task*
The efficient leader,
- is clear what his task is and understands how it fits into the long-term and short-term objectives of the organization,
- plans how to accomplish it,
- defines and provides the resources needed,
- ensures that each member of the group has clearly defined targets for improving performance,
- plugs any gaps in the abilities of the group by training and development,
- constantly evaluates results and monitors progress towards the goals.

(b) *Getting the best out of each individual*
He will see that each person,

29

- gets a sense of personal achievement in his job,
- feels he is making a worthwhile contribution,
- if his performance is unsatisfactory is told in what way and given help to improve,
- feels that his job challenges him and his capabilities are matched by the responsibilities given him,
- receives adequate recognition for his achievements, etc., etc.

(c) *Keeping high group morale*

The leader,
- provides regular opportunities for briefing the group,
- provides regular opportunities for genuine consultation before reaching decisions affecting them,
- accords the official representative of the group the facilities he needs to be its effective spokesman,
- ensures that there is a formal and fair grievance procedure understood by all, etc.

Actions of the leader in one area of need affect other areas. Defining and achieving objectives will not only help in getting the job done, it will also help ensure high group morale and get maximum commitment from individuals.

When the course is being run for the managers of a particular company or organization, the tutor here may well wish to bring out the practical implications of ACL in the special situation of the organization. For one, it may be the urgent need for each person to agree with his boss his main objectives, standards of performance, and targets for improvement. For another, it may be the need for briefing groups. For another, the right use of delegation or an exercise in job-enrichment, making the job more worthwhile.

To provide the right climate in which the opportunities for these needs can be met for each member of the group is probably the most difficult but certainly the most challenging and rewarding task of the leader.

Sessions Ten and Eleven. At this stage of the course the aim of these sessions is to give course members an opportunity to apply the practical implications of leadership, as studied in the last session, to a case study designed to simulate their normal job situation.

The case study is designed according to whether course members are from a commercial, industrial, or other background. A situation which has been found successful for those in industry or business concerns the trace-metal extraction division of a chemical company. The division has recently been engaging the attention of the group managing director on several counts : not the least being its steadily declining profits. A year or so ago the division was the subject of a study by consultants and a brief report of their findings and notes on the persons in the case are available.

Depending on the level of experience of course members a situation is contrived where groups of members are charged with being either the newly appointed general manager or the newly appointed production manager and briefed with the job of reporting to the group managing director on their plan of actions to be taken on taking up their new responsibilities.

The two groups of eight members are each observed by a team of two or three observers, who, without taking part in the discussion are observing and examining the findings of the team in the light of the three areas of leadership – the task, the group, and the individuals concerned.

During the reporting-back session each group explains the actions it will take on assuming office and, most important, the reasons for so doing. Immediately after each group report the associated observers give their analysis of the group's discussions and the management decisions recommended with special reference to the three areas of need. They are encouraged to probe along the lines :

'Will the group's recommended actions lead to achieving the desired task of bringing the division back into a viable state? Was this task clearly recognized and defined? Which actions should lead directly to meeting it? What steps have they suggested which should lead to improving morale in the division or department and to getting closer working among and within groups? Have the separate needs of the individuals in the case been met, as far as is possible in the present situation? How?'

In summary, the tutor comments on the groups' recommendations and also on the observers' analyses, drawing out the main lessons, revealing the opportunities missed by the groups, the matters undetected by both the groups and observers. A down-to-earth dialogue ensures that the practical actions which a leader must take in such a likely situation are recognized and understood.

'Is this new leader going to met the needs in the situation, the group needs and the individual needs? Has he achieved the right balance between the needs to enable him not only to show immediate results but to achieve these consistently and in the long term? Has he got his priorities right? Has he ensured that in the urgency to re-organize, the importance of reducing costs and improving morale, housekeeping, and liaison within and between departments is not overlooked? Is he going to succeed?'

Session Twelve. The final session is one of personal commitment.

Course members are given further practical help in being effective leaders in the industrial, commercial, or service situation by summarizing functional leadership in terms of the actions they will each take on return to their jobs arising from their course experience.

The course is divided into groups of not more than six members. These groups then spend 30 minutes discussing the individual actions each member intends to take on his return from the course. The chairman of each group ensures that each member is helped to an accurate solution of his problems and to seeing where lie the opportunities for his leadership in terms of actions he may take. Each group then chooses the three or four best 'actions' which are then displayed and discussed in plenary session.

In a final summary of the course the tutor points out that it would be quite wrong to imply however that simply going through the motions just listed will make a leader out of everyone. The 'person' of the leader, his 'humanity' as well as his actions, is an essential part of the formula which makes a man an effective leader. A better word for this is integrity, in the sense of the 'wholeness and wholesomeness' of the man.

This integrity is best seen reflected in the sort of comment made about a respected manager who is also a successful leader. For example:

- He is 'human' and treats us as human beings.
- Doesn't bear grudges; has no favourites; is fair to us as well as the company.
- He is easy to talk to and he listens—you can tell he listens.
- He is honest; keeps his word; doesn't dodge unpleasant issues.
- Drives himself hard—you don't mind him expecting the best of you.

The course is now finally summarized.
The job of the leader is:

- To ensure that the group works well together.
- To get the required results.
- To get each individual playing his maximum part.

32

These are the functions of the leader—the 'work' a manager has to perform to be a successful leader.

These are not inborn traits. They are skills which can be recognized, practised, and developed. A manager becomes a better leader when he improves his skills in these areas. How are YOU going to apply these ideas? What actions are YOU going to take back on the job?

3. ACL at work

In this chapter we look at four case studies of the application of ACL in the United Kingdom.

Ray Shaw, group training manager with Fisons Ltd, begins by describing one of the first adaptions of the approach based on Edwin Smith's tutor's manual. His contribution underlines the freedom enjoyed by those who adopt ACL as a training method, as far as its name and exercises are concerned, provided always that they maintain the essential content and training principles of the approach.

In fact, Ray Shaw and his colleagues have shown much creative thinking in evolving alternative and supplementary practical exercises for their course; exercises which they have shared with other users of ACL through The Industrial Society's annual Progress Conference, quarterly workshops on training methods, and Newsletter.

Especially interesting is his description of the careful pre-introduction testing of the course, and the steps taken to involve senior management in the success of the programme.

John Adair

Fisons Limited

Ray Shaw

Fisons is a medium-sized chemical group whose main manufacturing and marketing activities are in pharmaceuticals and toiletries, chemicals, and agricultural fertilizers. The group employs 8000 people, and its trading activities are carried out in three autonomous operating divisions: pharmaceutical, agro-chemical, and fertilizer. These operations are carried out in some 30 main units spread geographically over Great Britain.

Typical of the chemical industry, Fisons is capital intensive with relatively few people in a team for a given operation. Many managers and supervisors have only a few subordinates, and there is a relatively high ratio of managers and supervisors to other staff. For instance, many supervisors in Fisons have only three or four direct subordinates, each of whom is a specialist, having subordinates himself. So, in proportion to numbers employed, the Group has a high management training load. Each year five to six hundred people with managerial or executive responsibilities attend courses organized by the Group Training Department.

INTRODUCING LEADERSHIP TRAINING INTO FISONS

It is difficult to say which came first, the realization of the need for leadership training along the lines of ACL, or the realization that such a practical method of leadership training was available. In 1968, when we first learned of The Industrial Society's ACL courses we were already covering the general area of Motivation and Man Management on our supervisors' and managers' courses. Our treatment of this area was modern in the two senses that it was highly practical and participative, and that it covered much of the latest developments in both theory and practice, but there was something missing. It took some time to recognize what

D

this was and then only after we had run an ACL course. What had been missing was a simplified interpretation of the theories of the behavioural scientists to cover the need of the practical manager or supervisor with a team to lead, enthuse, direct, and inspire whilst himself beset by many pressures and problems, with little time or inclination to master the intricacies of industrial psychology.

The ACL course offered a simple, self-checking system to which a manager or supervisor could be introduced in a matter of hours and which he could then develop and build upon by experience and experiment in the work situation.

Other problem areas were beginning to emerge at this time, including the need for managers and supervisors to become more rational in their approach to problem solving. This, and other areas of which we were only just aware at the time, were highlighted by our later experience with ACL.

To summarize, we were attracted to ACL for three main reasons.

- It filled an emerging gap in our general repertoire of training for skills in management.
- It gave a simplified approach to leadership, reducing a hitherto woolly and diverse body of knowledge and opinion to a systematic functional style, or approach, to 'Man Management'. In doing so it also helped to remove the mystique from leadership (at the operational management level anyway!).
- It provided a simple system for self-analysis and self-improvement which was rapidly and easily learned, in a dramatic, practical and enjoyable manner.

STEPS IN TESTING ACL

First, we didn't like the title *Action-Centred Leadership*. This style of training is essentially 'practical', and we felt that 'Action Centred' tends to imply 'frenetic activity'. We wanted people to latch on to the 'practical' part, and we did not want them to forget that this approach to leadership relies as much on the 'thinking' and 'planning' activities as on the 'action'. So we called it simply *Practical Leadership*.

Our steps in initiating 'Practical Leadership' training were as follows:

Testing the Exercises. The training staff went through all the practical exercises described in the Industrial Society's ACL trainer's manual. This was done with the object of getting the feel of the exercises and to look for snags and likely areas of misunderstanding by leaders and by team

38

members. We then acted as tutors in running the exercises with leaders and teams made up from colleagues in other departments. These teams were carefully chosen so as to be representative of the mix of function and seniority we expected to find on our courses. Participants were not put into the exercises cold; we spent five minutes explaining that we were going through the exercises to gain experience ourselves and that we would welcome their comments and suggestions in an analysis session which would follow the exercise. We then spent about ten minutes giving them a lecturette on the 'leadership model'.

From these 'dry runs' we learned how to handle the exercises, we gained confidence and learned how participants were likely to react to the exercises. Reactions were generally favourable. For example we were pleasantly surprised to find that managers accepted the Mast Contract exercise at its face value and did not tend to see it as merely playing with Lego bricks. We then felt confident to try the course out.

Testing the Course. We carefully rearranged the programme of one of our supervisors' courses. By carefully pruning an hour or two of the least vital materials, and by working rather later on three days of this five-day course, we were able to find ten and a half hours to devote to Practical Leadership. We were able to cover a general introduction and discussion, 'The Functional Leadership Model', *Twelve O'Clock High* parts I and II, three exercises—'Planks and Drums', 'Jigsaws', and '£5000 Fund'—and 'Practical Implications of the Model'.

Reactions by participants were excellent, so much so that after the whole course finished on Friday, they went through 'Planks and Drums' again just to prove to themselves that it could be done well if the leader and group worked as a team.

Questioning what Improvements were needed. Our experience so far, and the reactions of those who had participated in parts of the course we had been able to test, led us to the following questions and conclusions

We needed some method of repeating the exercises. It is well-established practice in training to enable participants to improve their skill by trying out an exercise, noting their mistakes, and trying out the same exercise again. When we asked the question 'if you were to repeat the exercise, what would you do differently and why?' replies indicated that participants were learning from their mistakes and were keen to run through the exercise again to apply what they had learned.

We therefore developed variations on the standard exercises. For example, for a second run through 'Planks and Drums' we supplied a ten-foot plank which would not bear a person's weight; for a second run at 'Jigsaws' we supplied a third puzzle of similar manufacture and picture subject, but made of slightly thicker material. A variation of the 'Mast Contract' offered a proportionately greater 'profit' above a reasonably achievable height. Does the team go for a 'safe' objective or do they carry out investigational work to try to achieve the more difficult and coincidentally more rewarding objective? These variants of the original exercises had the same parameters and objectives but had different constraints. The next team therefore gained little from the problems solved by the previous team but were able to use the knowledge they had gained in analysing the previous team's successes and mistakes in functional leadership.

Quite early in our examination of ACL training as a technique it became obvious that unless we put emphasis in the right place managers would be likely to see leadership in a neutral or even negative way rather than in the desirable positive way. For example, we discovered participants could become engrossed in understanding people, in being able to translate and summarize the group's feelings and opinions, in resolving conflict, and generally in seeking 'comfort' for team members through group maintenance and individual fulfilment. But we wanted leaders who would ask questions likely to produce a set of sound alternative courses. We wanted leaders capable of extracting from the complex parameters and constraints a practicable objective to be met by the group. We wanted leaders to encourage promising ideas from their group, to prod and shock them into a creative, bold, and imaginative approach to their task. We felt that the leader would achieve this not by simply resolving conflict, but by controlling it, adding a little here to stimulate conflict and hence creativity, reducing it there so that the group could review progress and rethink its approach to its problems.

Introducing Practical Leadership in Fisons. We first met the technique of ACL training in November 1968. In early May 1969 we tested the course as described by inserting a large section of the technique into a supervisors' course and in mid-May we held a one-day presentation to about 20 top managers and training and personnel managers. The presentation took the form of a shortened version of the complete course with participants analysing *Twelve O'Clock High* then working through the 'Mast Contract'. This was followed by a description of the remaining exercises and a discussion on the possible use of the technique.

40

The reaction was excellent. After the presentation we received a round of applause—that doesn't happen very often in management training! Managers spoke of the course as being 'a revelation'—'we hadn't thought of leadership in quite that way' was a typical reaction. Top managers representing one Division demanded that we start right away in training all their management team from directors to chargehands! We have not quite managed that yet, but we have gone a long way towards it. Their reaction to *Twelve O'Clock High* was that although the American idiom caused them difficulties it was obvious that many ideas illustrated by the film were applicable in everyday life. 'Was the film made for leadership training?' is a question we were asked then and have been asked many time since.

Following this presentation we arranged to include Practical Leadership courses in our regular programme of courses. We ran the first of these courses at the end of May 1969 and we have run eleven more since. It seems that our programme for the future will be for four to six such courses a year. We run separate courses for managers and supervisors. The course for supervisors is three days, that for managers two days. We fix the maximum number of members as 15 with the ideal at 12. This ensures high participation and gives everyone several opportunities to be a team member for the exercises, and the majority to be a leader for an exercise.

General Conclusions. Participants are asked for their reactions to the course about six weeks after attending. They complete a simple questionnaire asking them to rate changes in their performance as leaders, and in their team's performance. To keep it simple these ratings are on a four-point scale of 'worse', 'same', 'better', 'much better'. Most ratings are 'better' or 'much better' for six factors in leadership, including motivation of the team, defining objectives, general team efficiency. This assessment is admittedly subjective, but it indicates that people feel that this approach to leadership is useful and worthwhile. Those who attend the course usually nominate subordinates, and often persuade their superiors to attend. No one would claim that the course is likely to result in revolutionary improvements in leadership but we believe that it fulfils a need. For too long people in managerial and supervisory positions have been harangued on the need for better 'human relations', with its inbuilt connotation of 'if you will only be nice to people they are likely to be nice back'. This course does much to demonstrate that this is not enough. It also demonstrates that whilst people are complex, difficult to understand,

41

and apparently irrational at times, it is possible to adopt and develop a systematic personal approach to enthusing them, interesting them in their often unpleasant and boring tasks and, in short, to make their working lives richer and more rewarding. This being to the mutual benefit of the organization and to the individual, not to mention the leader.

Participants won't remember all they have learned, they will probably forget quite a lot, but their reactions indicate they are still thinking about it several weeks after attending. It seems reasonable to suppose that they are practising what they remember; that they are building their own approach within the simple framework of functional leadership. Informal conversations we have with them from time to time support this view.

Having adapted and developed the course it is now a routine 'module' included in our range of courses. It is now regarded by management as a useful means of improving understanding and skill in leadership. We shall go on improving the course; there is a need for a still wider range of exercises; we need to give people more information on choice of leadership style to suit particular personalities and situations. Other improvements will also come no doubt. Finally, this course has been useful in indicating to participants and to tutoring staff other areas requiring detailed study and practice along similar participative lines.

In 1968, the managing director of the Bank of Ireland invited me to visit Dublin to explore the possibility that my approach to leadership training might be relevant to the banking situation. During this visit I spent some time in five branches, ranging from a large city bank to one in a small Irish county town where horse-drawn carts still wandered leisurely down the main street. My conversations with 60 or more members of staff convinced me that (in a suitably adapted form) the concept of functional leadership was indeed relevant; that the two-day courses and follow-up practical training described elsewhere in this book would make a valuable contribution to the development of management potential in the world of commerce.

Not so many years later, this judgement has been confirmed by some of the commercial organizations which have adopted ACL. The Industrial Society employed the ACL concept and methods in their courses for the Bank of England from the start, but several other major banks have since introduced ACL training into their organizations.

In the second contribution Mr F. J. Peacock, formerly responsible for management development in the personnel division of the National Westminster Bank, describes one such application. Besides commenting on the effectiveness of some parts of the course, Mr Peacock raises again some pertinent questions about evaluation.

John Adair

National Westminster Bank Limited

F. J. Peacock

The National Westminster Bank, as such, came into being on 1 January 1970; before that, the three major banks involved in the merger—District, National Provincial, and Westminster—had carried on in their traditional ways, even in some places to the extent of a splendid reluctance to abandon the competitive habits of a managerial lifetime.

Apart from the associated companies in the Group, the new bank, with probably the biggest network of any bank in the world, has six functional divisions and three operational divisions of which one, Domestic Banking, consists of seven Regions divided into 80 areas employing two-thirds of the Group's total staff. On the domestic front there are 2334 full branches, 3619 offices in all and a staff of 52 000 of whom 50 per cent are women. Of that 50 per cent the majority are of comparatively brief experience, for the Bank in common with many large-scale organizations today, is particularly vulnerable to the restless ways of the young in a society committed to full employment. Two-thirds of its staff are in branches so that the bulk of its operations are carried out in towns and cities where there are often problems arising from catering difficulties, travelling, housing problems and the like.

Branches have increased in number, a feature which has inevitably thrown a strain on supervisory resources and the reservoir of managerial potential, in an industry which does little recruiting at mature levels and prides itself on growing its own managerial timber. Established branches increased in size as the number of account holders grew and the range of services offered attracted wider acceptance. Such pressures in a number of places have led to a split organization of a work force on more than

45

one level, to a departmentalized or sectionalized structure in large and even medium-sized branches, to operations being removed from the public area to the seclusion of back offices or adjacent premises.

Fortunately, despite differences in systems and company traditions, there was no difference in outlook between the three Banks in their basic attitude towards training although there were, as might be expected, differences in the timing of courses, the editing of course content, and the commitment to the various media available. With the merger, all activities were reviewed and a comprehensive programme from Induction to Managerial seminars designed to take advantage of the best features from the constituent Banks' past practices and experience.

Why we Adopted ACL. The concept of action-centred leadership not only made sense, but it made attractive good sense. It gave promise of a more exciting and therefore more interesting way of passing on to young people the knowledge and understanding of working relationships that they need to progress along the managerial path. We believed that it could be adapted and translated into specific banking settings so that the lessons could be learned with vivid and lasting effect. We recognized it as a valuable reinforcement of our various in-company training measures. We had case studies, syndicate discussions, films, film strips and so on. But there was a continuing need to highlight the need for conscious positive leadership, especially in the branch or section setting where the members of a working group could be under many pressures. We had plenty of experience of 'bad' branches where leadership had proved inadequate, and we knew why. Equally, we had success stories where a strategic change in a key post had brought cohesion and confidence to a dispirited band of capable people who were losing faith in their own capabilities. We decided, therefore, 'to read on'.

ACL IN ACTION

The senior tutor of one of our residential training centres reports:

❝ We first introduced action-centred leadership in January 1970, using the film *Twelve O'Clock High* in three-week residential courses for senior Sub-Managers who should all be nearing appointment as Managers. Of the 400 men who have been through this form of training, some 50 have also participated in a practical exercise similar to the £5000 Endowment Fund, but based on a banking situation.

We have also incorporated the concept in a two-week development course for men in the 23 to 29 age group, assessed by the Bank as having the potential for senior managerial responsibility. In two courses, 30 members on each have been involved in a one-day session on two exercises, again similar to the Endowment Fund but using situations in a banking context. On these occasions we used the 'Endowment Fund' as an opener, with a demonstration by Tutors.

In the course for senior men, the film has been used right at the beginning, to awaken the awareness of members to the overall field of leadership, with specific aspects such as delegation and communication examined in greater depth in subsequent course session.**"**

We are reluctant, particularly in the 'Senior' courses, to introduce some of the exercises, the Mast Contract for instance, because we find that there is a greater appreciation of the issues involved if relation can be made to the working environment in which the members operate. Having decided to extend ACL training to include practical exercises, we therefore produced two cases of our own, both in a banking context, one of them dealing with a staff problem. One requires six role-players, the other four—including the leader in each case. Working groups comprise 12 members, so a number of people take the observer role. The subsequent discussions are given more structure and point by using observer sheets, with the various responsibilities collated into task group and individual needs.

In the discussion on these areas of need we always refer to the Blake/Mouton Grid, to Maslow's hierachy of needs (in rather more detail) and also to the various styles of leadership in their subordinate involvement in decision-making. We are conscious of the need to keep course members, in the observers' comments which follow and in the discussion generally, off the problem AS a problem and ON leadership aspects. We find that great care is necessary in choosing the leader for, if the exercise is to be of real benefit, his leadership is going to be the subject of specific comment—not all of it favourable—after the role-playing.

Evaluation is something on which we hesitate to speak with certainty. Courses are 'evaluated' in terms of an anonymous written feedback from members at the end, which in itself is not a reliable evaluation pointer in terms of the objectives of the ACL sessions; these objectives are broadly as set out in the manual. Also, our review is of the total (two- or three-week) course of which ACL concepts form only a part. From this review and the verbal feedback which we receive, the ACL sessions have always been well received; in the reviews themselves, the leadership studies are often mentioned as,

- a part of the course having the greatest value;
- one of the areas in which course members intend to give attention to their own performance back on the job.

We find the ACL concept extremely useful, particularly in courses where the overall field of management is explored in detail. Also (and this is important) our tutors, who generally have had practical experience of management in the Bank, are themselves helped to understand the leadership role better.

We are working on a method of objective evaluation of the extent to which performance back on the job has been improved by the course as a whole.

At the close of our courses, there is always a formal dinner arranged by the members themselves. Generally, they adopt a particular theme for the evening as a whole and for their speeches in particular. That the ACL vehicle has made an impact can be seen from the fact that the senior course have sometimes taken their theme from the *Twelve O'Clock High* film, role-playing the dinner as a reunion of 918 Squadron.

The course has been running for 12 months now and tutors are finding that, for them, the film *Twelve O'Clock High* has lost its first fine careless rapture and is fast becoming a bore. On the other hand, each new course finds the film an attractive and effective introduction. The search for an alternative film continues and must succeed if we are to avoid action-centred mutiny among the tutors!

From another residential centre, which had passed 140 students, rather younger and one rung down the seniority ladder from their colleagues above, comes the following comments.

ff Thus far, there have been no formal attempts to evaluate ACL sessions separately from other parts of the course. General comments are favourable and for most people there is attraction in activities such as the 'Mast Contract', completely unrelated to banking in day-to-day terms, which highlight general principles valid in varying situations.

Unfortunately we cannot associate with the course a 'before and after' questionnaire on leadership performance because of movement from branch to branch of students and reporting officers, or because of changes in the group supervised. It is possible, however, to nominate for attendance on such courses as these—externally usually—men and women whose performance has been criticized or is in any way suspect. Thereafter a specific follow-up can be made and this has been done with excellent results. In one case an able man had taken over what he felt to be a badly run and loosely disciplined office. His efforts to change the scene had been ill received by the staff and criticized, not altogether justly, by other senior officers. A leadership course gave him the opportunity to reassess his problems, to reconsider the appropriateness of his methods and to sit in judgement on his past performance. The functional approach to leadership had its lessons for him and with a new approach he should be able to create conditions in which those who work with him can learn by example and enjoy the day's work in the process.**"**

Conclusion. Despite the difficulties of evaluation and marked variation in student reaction, we have faith in the ACL approach and it will continue to form part of our management development courses when they are re-established in our new large and comprehensive centre. With new entrants and trainee managers on the same site we could develop a combined exercise and variant on the present activity. It will be interesting to try.

Certainly there will be no lessening of the need to induce men and women who have a claim to promotion by enthusiasm and technical competence in support roles, to think hard about the nature of leadership and the demands that will be made on them if they are to be effective and acceptable both to higher authority and, perhaps more importantly, to those who look to them for guidance, support and task satisfaction.

Almost every branch of the public services has shown interest in ACL training during the past four years. The Prison Service, for example, has used the course for training prison officers and the Police College at Bramshill was among the first to include lectures and the film Twelve O'Clock High in their programme. For the general social and economic factors which have led to the need for a high quality of leadership at many levels in organizational life are by no means confined to industry and commerce. They influence every organization—government, church, or service—in the public sector.

The medical profession has experienced this feature of social change. The doctors' role, in hospital or general practice, can be seen as demanding a degree of leadership. The Report of the Royal Commission on Medical Education (1965–1968) stressed it:

'The increasing need for the doctor to work in close co-operation, both in diagnosis and therapy, with people who are not medically qualified—not only with the scientists whose contribution to clinical assessment is becoming increasingly important, but also with many others who have important responsibilities for the patient both in ancillary services and in other capacities, and above all with the patient himself—a patient better informed and more interested in science and medicine than some doctors have often encountered hitherto. The leadership which the doctor often has to exercise has sometimes in the past appeared to be based on the assumption of a charismatic authority which has already ceased to be convincing and in the future will be completely inappropriate. The basis of the doctor's leadership will be his superior knowledge of the central facts of the clinical situation, his ability to exercise a decisive influence on the patient's illness, and his capacity to guide and co-ordinate the work of others whose co-operation is essential.'

Thus the hospitals and medical services can be seen as human organizations requiring a high quality of leadership if they are to achieve their distinctive purposes. But, if so, the traditional methods for training may not be sufficient, especially in the human side of hospital management. The Senior Assistant Regional Training Officer of the South-East Metropolitan Regional Hospital Board, Mr W. J. Owens, SRN, RNMS, RNT, suggests in the third contribution what considerable advances can be made in this vitally important field.

John Adair

South-East Metropolitan Hospital Board

W. J. Owens

In July 1963, the Minister of Health appointed a committee under the chairmanship of Sir Brian Salmon to 'advise on the Senior Nursing Staff structure in the Hospital Service—the administrative functions of the respective grades, and the methods of preparing staff to occupy them'.

The subsequent *Report of the Committee on Senior Nursing Staff Structure* (HMSO 1966) recommended what amounted to :

> 'a major organizational change in the pattern of nursing administration—from a rigid authoritarian approach where authority remained with one person, the Matron, in each hospital, to a decentralized functional structure of delegated responsibility and authority for all the hospitals, under a Hospital Management Committee's control.'

The report stated : 'We are aware that these changes we recommend cannot be implemented unless nurses are educated to the jobs we describe. Accordingly, we have proposed a broad scheme of systematic education and training for promotion upward through first line to top management, with the accent upon progressively increasing management skills.'

The report was accepted, and in 1968 the National Nursing Staff Committee recommended that Regional Hospital Boards should make provision for management training for senior nurses, Deputy and Assistant Matrons, and male equivalents. In June 1969, the S.E. Metropolitan Hospital Board drafted a programme covering the syllabus recommended by the National Nursing Staff Committee. The courses would be of four weeks' duration, based on the sandwich principle : phase A lasting two weeks, followed by eight weeks back in the work situation, then back for two weeks of phase B.

As the first course was scheduled to start in September 1969, it was not possible to identify needs systematically before formulating aims and constructing the course programme. Instead, various facts were established and a number of assumptions made. The assumptions were :

- That there would be a wide disparity of occupation in terms of task, responsibility, authority, and performance.
- That the following strengths and weaknesses were likely to exist :

Strengths	Weaknesses
Enormous goodwill	Traditional attitudes and approach
An intense desire to learn	Inhibition
Nursing training and qualifications	Lack of imagination
	Ill-defined tasks and responsibilities
Comparable experience at ward level	Ineffectiveness, because the students would not have been encouraged
Maturity	to use their own initiative

These assumptions were subsequently proved to be correct.

After much thought and discussion the course aims were defined as helping students to :

- develop as individuals,
- master certain skills associated with middle management,
- enable them to fill their existing and developing roles more fully.

Studying these specific aims, it was clear that in view of the original assumptions particular attention would have to be paid to the students' roles as leaders in the work situation.

Why ACL? The traditional approach to leadership training in the Nursing profession is the 'qualities' approach : throughout the training period great stress is placed on loyalty, integrity, obedience, and so on. However, there are some remarkable omissions. For example, initiative is very much frowned upon—summed up in the once well-used phrase, 'Nurse, you are not paid to think'. It was therefore necessary to develop a different approach to leadership training; one that was sufficiently dramatic to make a real and lasting impact.

The Regional Training Officer was at that time developing a construction project, using building kits, in which unstructured groups of students were faced with the task of producing under certain conditions a replica of a master model. While the groups were engaged in this task, observers recorded the activities and group interactions that occurred. The objective was to analyse the behaviour patterns exhibited by the group and to equate such behaviour to performance.

We had used this project, with encouraging results, when the writer attended a one-day Action-Centred Leadership Tutors' Course organized by The Industrial Society. The day was fruitful, because the two-day programme seemed to be the very thing we were looking for, and with slight amendment could be introduced into phase A of our course, as an integral element of the programme. All the work in the first week would lead up to a natural introduction to ACL and the lessons learned during the module and the uses of the approach could be applied to subsequent course work. In this way, a pattern of leadership behaviour could be developed and applied back in the working situation with considerable benefit.

The course programme for this particular module is as follows :

Monday	Tuesday
11 a.m.–12.30 p.m. Construction Project (by unstructured group), followed by analysis and discussion of group behaviour patterns.	**9.30–10.45 a.m.** Leadership Film I, analysis and discussion.
1.45–3.15 p.m. Introduction and Development of the Functional Leadership Model.	**11 a.m.–12.30 p.m.** Leadership Film II, analysis and discussion.
3.45–5.15 p.m. Case Study I The £5000 Fund, analysis and discussion (adapted for the Hospital Service).	**1.45–3.15 p.m.** 'The Mast Contract', analysis and discussion. **3.45–5.15 p.m.** Practical implications.

In addition, every subsequent course exercise is monitored by observers who report on the syndicates' effectiveness and relate it to the use made of the leadership approach.

Evaluation. We have been using this element of training since September 1969, and have attempted to evaluate the benefit in a variety of ways :

- Session evaluation forms were completed by students who were asked to rate the session on a five-point value basis. Over 85 per cent of the students gave it top rating with an extremely high application value.

- Interviews have been held with the senior officers of a random selection of former course members. The results of these interviews have been most encouraging, senior officers in some cases reporting 'absolutely dramatic' improvement to 'noticeable' improvement. 'No improvement' was reported in 12 per cent of the sample, but the course tutor noted in half of these interviews a varying degree of disapproval of the *principles* of Functional Leadership.
- All students are invited back to the Centre three to nine months after completion of the course. During the day they submit to the course tutors, their colleagues, and a number of invited senior officers a verbal report on 'the difficulties I encountered on return to the working situation, and the action I have taken to overcome them.'

These report-back days have been very encouraging, and the students have been ever-ready to pay tribute to the advantages of the ACL approach.

One Nursing Officer reported :

66 Before I attended the course I was quite frankly in a rut. I was in charge of a Geriatric Long-stay Hospital of 73 beds. The hospital was in fact built as a workhouse in the reign of Queen Victoria. Staff were difficult to recruit, and even more difficult to keep. The patients, all of them old, many mentally confused, led an uneventful twilight existence, virtually awaiting death as a happy release.

After the module on Action-Centred Leadership I asked myself why I had never thought of myself as a positive leader of staff and patients. I do not to this day know the answer. However, I resolved that when I got back things would be different.

A week after my return I forced myself to define my task. I now saw it as a home provider for my patients and being responsible for providing a stimulating environment as far as I could. This led me to set up a meeting to put these ideas to the staff and invite suggestions as to how we could develop them. At the end of the meeting I had three groups of staff working on three different areas of activity, and I am happy to report the following :

- Patients able and willing to potter about the gardens have their own flower beds, pot plants, or flower boxes. The staff have modified small gardening tools so that they can be manipulated from wheel-chairs, etc.
- Coach rides for the patients have been organized, the cost being

partially defrayed by the League of Friends. Picnics have been held for patients and their relatives in the hospital grounds.

- Another group undertook to encourage local bodies to take an interest in the hospital and its patients. This has resulted in local Music and Drama groups coming into the hospital to provide, on a regular basis, Music and Drama evenings.

- A third group enlisted the help of fifth and sixth formers from the local Grammar School. This has resulted in 'adoptions' by groups of scholars, and two patients go to the College each Friday during term and lunch with a party of students and masters. The students organize all the transport and entertainment.

These activities have transformed the environment of the hospital.

During the past six months, staff wastage has been reduced to nil; the patients are much more aware of their surroundings and are, as one nurse put it, much more interesting people; and the Night Sedation bill has been reduced by £300."

Another Senior Nurse reported that she had used the ACL approach to bring together the Ward Sisters of a hospital which consisted of two wings—one opened in 1882 and the other in 1969. By a process of group selection she formed teams of ward sisters to study particular areas of ward management in both old and new locations and to make recommendations on 'Best Practice'. This turned 'a charming bunch of fiercely individualistic sisters into an effective team of ward managers'.

On each of the report-back days, the question of leadership was constantly referred to, and without exception students stressed how different their approach now was.

"Although I had been a leader for some time before the course, subsequent practice and the different results I get now prove how inadequate I was twelve months ago."

"I went back to the work situation quietly determined to apply the lessons I'd learned. By harnessing the individual abilities of my staff into an effective team, we transformed our department. Unfortunately for me, my Senior Officer then asked me to take over and reorganize another department. By using the ACL approach we managed to produce some very effective changes, and now I am used as a 'trouble shooter'."

"For eighteen years, I had been instructed: 'I want you to do this, I want you to do that', and frankly this was my own approach with subordinates. But by using this Functional Leadership approach I find I am getting far better results from subordinates; we, as a team, are now capable of coping with a volume of work which I would have thought impossible twelve months ago.**"**

This is just a small selection of quotable reports. We have, in fact, a great deal of evidence that much more effective leadership is now being practised by middle managers. This may in fact have produced problems for nurses further up the ladder, occupying top-line management positions. Middle managers who have taken the ACL module are now looking for much more positive leadership by their seniors. When it comes to these more senior managers, ex-students expect them to adopt the 'needs approach' and are often frustrated when it is not forthcoming.*

* The last point made by W. J. Owens is a common one. Organizations are like the human body; if a change takes place in one 'member' it influences the other members or organs. In the short term it is necessary for the tutor to stress the positive actions that anyone at any level can take to improve his own leadership performance, regardless of what is happening above or below him. In the longer term, however, only an improvement in leadership at all levels will bring about those marked and significant improvements in organizational performance and unity, while also promoting the maximum use of human resources and the fullest possible job satisfaction for individuals, which are so vital for our day and age.

The first research visits, field studies, and course experiments in the ACL approach to leadership took place in 1962. The short, concentrated thirty-six-hour course has been operational at Sandhurst since 1964. Besides spreading by a natural process to the Royal Air Force and the Royal Navy, its use has also widened in the Army. For example, the basic concepts and methods of the approach are now required reading for the Army's Promotion and Staff College examinations, which all officers sit in their late twenties, and they feature as part of the Staff College syllabus. Indeed all three Service Staff Colleges now included lectures and studies on the Functional Leadership approach in their programmes. Since Arthur Adamson completed his article, the Royal Marines have adopted this approach in their officer and non-commissioned officer training schools.

Wing Commander Arthur Adamson RAF presents as the fourth 'case history' an overall picture of what has happened in the British Armed Forces. As senior education officer at the RAF Officer Cadet Training Unit, he played a prominent part in one of the most successful applications of functional leadership theory and methods to the practical problem of developing the leadership potential of new officers. Having visited the Unit myself several times, and studied the evaluation results and met some of the over 1500 officer cadets of all branches, ages, and functions who had by then passed through the Functional Leadership course, I became deeply impressed by the enthusiastic and professional approach of Wing Commander Adamson and his colleagues.

As explained earlier, Functional Leadership (FL) and Action-Centred Leadership (ACL) are interchangeable terms; FL being used in the Armed Services and ACL by The Industrial Society.

John Adair

The British Armed Services

Arthur Adamson

The importance of leadership in military organizations is well documented. Its vital contribution in times of crisis and action has been much emphasized, and military leaders are thought of in terms of drive, toughness, and decisive action. But much of military life is humdrum, and morale (unless husbanded by intelligent leadership) can be eroded by frustration and boredom. A military leader has to be able to cope with both action and monotony—and the latter perhaps calls for the greater ability.

This section is concerned with junior leaders at the start of their service careers, before they start to practise the profession of military leadership. It is therefore appropriate to consider the responsibilities of junior commanders:

- Their decisions often have to be made in an environment of crisis and uncertainty.
- Their decisions may have far-reaching effects, beyond their immediate command; even in an internal security situation a junior commander could make a mistake that could touch off civil strife.
- Responsibility comes early in life; an infantry platoon commander aged 19 has nearly 40 men under him.
- Their responsibility is for 24 hours of the day, and often extends to the families of those whom they lead.
- They have little control over the financial rewards of those they lead. The loss of this important motivational factor has to be offset by providing psychological satisfaction.

- They have the advantage of leading in a disciplined organization, with the support of a strong code of conduct and tradition of service.

In the Army, an officer may be in a fighting arm or a technical service, but in either he will command a number of men, often in an uncomfortable environment in peace, and certainly in a hostile situation in war.

In the Royal Air Force there are two major categories of junior officers: *aircrew* officers who lead, or who are members of small, closely-knit groups made up of individuals of similar ability, and where an understanding of the process of leadership and group interaction is vital; and *ground* officers who control relatively large numbers of highly trained men.

In the Royal Navy, a junior officer may be a seaman, engineer, or another kind of specialist responsible for a department providing a distinctive function on board ship. In addition he may be a divisional officer responsible for the welfare and control of men when they are not on duty in operational departments, and have secondary duties concerned with sports, entertainment, or other amenities.

Officers in all three services need specialist knowledge to cope with technological advances. But the improved education and skills of those they lead, and changing social attitudes, require them also to exercise leadership ability based on an understanding of human relationships, as well as upon their rank and technical knowledge.

The selection of candidates for officer training is based on two factors:

Attainment. Educational standards are set to indicate potential for learning. These are increasing, in direct competition with further education outside the services, and with the universities. In some cases attainment proved by executive experience is accepted, including successful non-commissioned service.

Personal qualities. Evidence is required that the candidate has personal qualities and attributes which are appropriate to the particular service. These include courage, physical fitness, intelligence, integrity, and the ability to work in cooperation with others. Additional qualities are required for specialist appointments.

The quality of those selected has a direct bearing on the methods by which they are trained. The highly critical faculties and complex motives of young people now entering the Armed Services lead them to expect and appreciate relevance, credibility, and efficiency in their training.

The Functional Leadership Introductory Course. Five basic training units use the Functional Leadership training at present and, by their diversity, give an overall picture of what is happening in the British Armed Services. They are :

Royal Military Academy, Sandhurst (RMAS),
Royal Air Force College, Cranwell,
Royal Air Force Officer Cadet Training Unit, Henlow (RAF OCTU),
Royal Navy Special Duties Officers School, Eastney (RN SDOS),
Royal Air Force Airmen Aircrew Initial Training Course, Topcliffe
    (RAF AAITC).

All these units use the one-and-a-half-day introductory course designed originally at RMAS and which reached its developed form in 1964. Students take an introductory course in classes of about 20, each with a trained instructor. The instructors are experienced leaders of the rank of major or its equivalent. Students are separated from all other distractions for the one and a half days of the course, and for a proportion of each session they work in unsupervised syndicates of four or five persons.
The pattern of the course is basically the same in all units :

Introduction: The students are set the question : 'What does a leader have to *do* to lead?' This stimulates thought and discussion about leadership and often reveals common misconceptions.

Leadership Theory and Observation Exercises: The Functional Leadership concept is introduced, and the class observes and analyses a series of short practical tasks to test it. These are performed in groups with a leader appointed to each group.

Leadership and Decision-making: Specific situational features of *military* leadership are introduced, and the extent to which subordinates may participate in decision-making is then discussed. The class is set the problem : 'What factors should a leader consider in determining how far he should share decision-making with his group?'

Film: The class use the Functional Leadership concept to analyse the film *Twelve O'Clock High*. This film demonstrates a high-stress operational situation in which one leader fails and is replaced by one who succeeds.

Exercise 'Remake': The class is given a case study of a small unit in a long-term peacetime situation. This is an FL analysis exercise in which

61

the class interprets the needs of the unit and then decides on what functions should be applied.

Conclusion: The class discusses and decides what has been learnt, what more the students need to know, and how they can apply what they have learnt. The aim is to reinforce learning and open up students' minds to subsequent practical leadership training. Each session has only a small amount of theory from the instructor, followed by problem-solving exercises in syndicates, and then by discussions involving the whole class. The instructor stays in the background and lets the students interact. At the end of each session and course, each student completes a 'reaction sheet', recording his opinion and a summary of the main points he has learnt. This serves two purposes : it recalls and reinforces learning, and provides feedback for development of the course. It has proved to be a useful and essential part of every course.

Practical Training. At each of the five units, the concept and methods of the short introductory course were gradually extended into the practical training phase in the remainder of the course. The Services enjoy an advantage here over other organizations that do not have a full-time course, as it enables their students to relate theory to leadership tasks which they will perform in operational service. In this phase the leadership training is symbiotic : it is conducted on exercises that are designed to train students for other professional skills demanded by their Service. Exercises are planned to give experience in all three areas of need. Leadership is briefed and debriefed separately from other techniques involved in the exercises, and with equal emphasis. The leadership training element follows a similar pattern in each of the units :

- Before the exercise the instructor outlines the situation and task, and the leader is invited to ask questions. The instructor clarifies the aims of the exercise and the lessons to be learnt, and reminds group members to observe and analyse FL needs and functions.
- During the exercise the leader is in complete control. The instructor intervenes only if the value of the exercise is being lost, or if there is danger to students.
- After the exercise :
  The leader gives his own opinion of the exercise and analyses his mistakes.
  The group discusses the needs that had arisen and the functions

that were available to meet them. They must 'speak to data'; that is, give positive statements to support opinions. It is essential to avoid a 'halo' effect about the exercise, and to identify specific than set good examples or reveal faults.

The instructor sums up to ensure that both leader and group have observed the main lessons.

In the early stages of practical training, students may be equipped with *aide-mémoire* cards, listing needs, functions, and key questions. These cards are superfluous once the concepts are well learnt.

The instructor must keep in mind a basic philosophy about this form of training:

- The aim is to bring about in the leader and in the group an *awareness* of needs, *understanding* of the appropriate functions, and *skill* in performing these functions.
- The leader gains skill from practising his functions while in command. The group, as observers and participants, gain awareness and understanding from their analysis.

This experience encourages students to express their opinions freely; learning comes from a free interplay of ideas with experiences. The instructor acts as a guide, summarizing and colouring the students' reactions with his own experienced comments.

Real Leadership Experience. All five units have found ways of applying leadership training to real task situations. Students are appointed, for a period of time, to be responsible for organizing and administering some aspect of domestic or training routine. Leadership and initiative projects are undertaken on a group basis. Social occasions are organized by students. Some units have introduced 'projects' as part of the training. At the RAF OCTU, for example, students in groups study a critical period in RAF history in terms of the major international, economic, technological, and social factors that affected the defence policy of the time. An important factor of the project is a series of presentations to all the other students on the course. All these situations present the appointed leader and his group with real task needs, and pose entirely different team maintenance and individual needs. The same process of debriefing and analysis are used for these real situations as for the training exercises.

Effect of FL Training on other aspects of training. The FL analysis of needs and functions has developed at some of the units into the identification and definition of the leadership functions required for the particular Service's environment. In varying degrees this has had effects on other aspects of training. It is best illustrated by the work at the RAF OCTU, where the functions were defined eventually as shown in Figure 3.1 below.

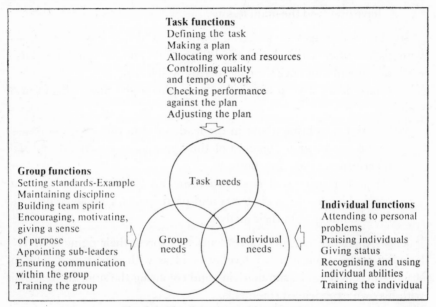

Fig. 3.1. The Functions of Leadership.

Defining functions provides a framework for job analysis of the leadership work of a junior officer. By looking at each function it is possible to decide which particular knowledge, skills, and attitudes will be needed to perform that function. It is then possible to decide the right emphasis to be given in the appropriate area of training, to set realistic objectives, and to establish the inter-relationship of various aspects of training. At the RAF OCTU, training in subjects like decision-making, controlling, communication, interviewing, counselling, welfare, and behavioural studies was remodelled on this analysis.

Effect on Training Methods. The one-and-a-half-day FL course was an innovation in leadership training because it introduced a new concept which explained what happened in a leadership situation. This had an important effect on basic military leadership training. However, the course was equally significant in that it took a new approach by making training sessions student-centred, with an instructor acting as an aid and guide.

64

Students learn from their experience of analysing and exercising command, but in the uninhibited exchange of ideas and opinions they gained insight through experiencing the reactions of fellow students; they appreciate the consequences of their own actions. In this respect the method appears to incorporate some of the better features of sensitivity training (T-Groups), without some of the unwelcome side-effects.

The freer participative approach did not relax standards; in fact, the transition of the instructor's role from driver to leader released the natural inclinations of students to set their own, ever higher, standards. A greater empathy was formed between students and instructor and the instructor could see more clearly the specific needs of individual students, concentrating his efforts on training rather than on assessment.

The successful student-centred method in FL training provided at most units a model and an opportunity to improve methods employed in other training areas. Anyone involved in adult education and training will appreciate how difficult it is to persuade some teachers away from the instructor-centred lecture approach. The evidence of the efficiency of student-centred learning, compared with instructor-centred training, led units to extend the method.

Reaction of those Involved in the Training. The first point at which it is possible to evaluate the effect of FL training is the reaction of those involved in it. The 'reaction sheet' mentioned earlier requires each student to record how he rated the training, on a nine-point scale :

1—unsatisfactory, 3—weak, 5—satisfactory, 7—good, 9—excellent.

All five units use the same system, and overall ratings have stood consistently between seven and eight for course after course.

In the training environment, the values represented by these ratings may not be other than subjective, but they do provide a valid yardstick for comparison purposes. Students have no inhibitions about rating a badly-designed or handled session low on the scale. This is invaluable information for the instructional staff in identifying areas for improvement of instructor training.

The reaction sheets also require students to identify those parts of the session they preferred, what in particular they had learnt, and any other comments they might wish to make. To the instructor, such remarks can have a salutary effect; to the controlling body they can be evidence on which to adjust content and method.

As an example, one of the regular courses at the RAF OCTU is for doctors, dentists, chaplains, nurses, and other professionally qualified entrants. They come to the training with their own mature experience, and with set professional attitudes. Some suspect that the Service wishes to impose on them values that are at odds with their professional ethics. The earlier courses reacted badly to FL training, rating it in the three–five area. On the basis of these ratings and students' remarks, gradual adjustments were made to attune training to their attitudes, and to relate exercises to leadership situations matched to their specializations. Ratings rose as detailed adjustments were made, until they settled at about the eight-level. One notable feature is that students who have received university level education are agreeably surprised to find the Services using a mature and adult approach in leadership training. They had expected to be told how to lead and instead, they found themselves in a process of problem-solving and free discussion with fellow students and instructors. This is relevant comment in these days of university students' clamour for more participation in the learning process.

The Services train as officers numbers of men who have seen service in the ranks and who have held executive posts as uncommissioned officers. Typical of their comments is: 'If I had had FL training when I first became an NCO, I would have made fewer mistakes.' Similar comments are made by mature men and women students who have come from executive experience in civilian life.

At the RAF OCTU, women are trained alongside men, and in many of the training exercises the groups and syndicates are 'mixed'. This appears to create few difficulties for the women, who are as capable as men in understanding and exercising leadership in mixed groups. In fact, the analytical approach offers distinct advantages in the leadership training of women. Instructors are selected from experienced leaders in the specializations represented among the students. Most instructors are enthusiastic about the FL concept, and they colour and develop it with their own experience. Over the past years, the system has come under the close scrutiny of many high-ranking Service officers: men who have amply demonstrated their own leadership ability. Without their approval it is unlikely that the system would have survived.

Given a constant selection standard for entry, and constant standards for commissioning, the efficiency of the training unit is reflected in the proportion of students who pass their training course successfully. Over the years, the Services have insisted on keeping their entry and commissioning standards at the same high levels. In recent years the success rates at RAF OCTU, especially among direct entrants from civilian life,

66

rose steadily. Senior officers at the unit attribute this principally to the introduction of FL training.

Effectiveness in Operational Units. A most valid point to consider in measuring the effectiveness of FL training is the performance in operational units of those who have undergone the training.

RMAS sent out questionnaires to a cross-section of officers, two years after they were commissioned (some of them on operational service overseas), asking them to comment on the value of leadership training. In the main they were encouraging and constructive in their comments. The RMAS also reports having received an increasing demand from within the Army for more information about Functional Leadership training; this is attributed to ex-students and instructors advertising its value when they join or rejoin their units.

RAF OCTU sends out similar questionnaires to ex-students who have been in operational service for a year or so. Many of them single out FL training as that part of the course that had proved particularly useful.

A third and most valid point on measurement is the effect on the total efficiency of an organization. This is difficult to detect and measure, because of the many factors that affect overall efficiency. It would be idle to claim, for instance, that FL training of even more than 12 000 young officers and SNCOs has had much measurable effect on the total efficiency of the Armed Forces. Leadership ability is still culled mainly from experience in commanding people in real situations, and most senior officers gained their considerable abilities in this way. What *can* be claimed is that the new generation of young officers, in a changing social and economic environment, are better equipped to undertake their first leadership jobs than they would have been without FL training. They have better understanding of the needs of the Service and those they command, and they have had better opportunities to practise the functions that are required to meet those needs. It can also be claimed that they have a better basis on which to develop future leadership abilities from their successes and failures in command. In the long term this must have a profitable effect for the Services.

At present, the FL approach to training ends with the basic course for commissioning. But lasting effects need constant refreshments, in the continuation training of officers, in specialist training courses, in promotion examination requirements, and in junior command and staff schools. There are signs that these developments will take place. For example, the

Army has included Functional Leadership in its officers' promotion examination syllabus.

Conclusions:
- Leadership training is an important part of the work of a military officer and is an important aspect of his basic training.
- FL training can improve leadership abilities; the individual's personal qualities are a basis for development.
- FL training is in keeping with the attitudes of the younger generation.
- Experienced leaders, especially trained, are essential to conduct FL training.
- FL learning is student-centred, coming from an interaction of observation and opinion. The instructor should aid and guide.
- The short introductory FL course has stood the test of time.
- The analysis process can be extended to real leadership tasks that arise in the training and administration of a training unit.
- The definition of functions can lead to a rationalization of other training aspects.
- A central controlling body is essential, to conduct research, develop methods, evaluate training, and train instructors. The best combination is a professional trainer with experienced practising leaders.
- Reaction ratings and students' comments are invaluable in adjusting content and method.
- FL training is invaluable to students who will become members of close-knit groups.
- Most instructors are enthusiastic about FL training; high-ranking officers give it their approval and mature and experienced students approve of the concepts and methods.
- There is no hard evidence yet that FL training has affected the overall efficiency of the Services. There is evidence, however, that young officers are better equipped to deal with present junior leadership conditions and also to develop their own leadership abilities.

4. The progress of ACL

The progress of ACL

The reader may already have partially constructed his mental outline of the history of ACL; this chapter is designed to fill in more of the details. For, in order to understand any phenomenon, it is useful to grasp the story of its growth and development.

In 1969, The Industrial Society undertook the responsibility of making Functional Leadership Training, on the Sandhurst model, available to industry, nationally and internationally. The Society's involvement had come about almost by chance. In 1966, the Personnel Director of the Imperial Tobacco Company sat in as observer on one of the Sandhurst courses. Being also on the Council of The Industrial Society, he reported on the course to the Society's director, John Garnett. After several meetings, and a lecture which I gave to a Society conference, The Industrial Society became steadily more committed to Functional Leadership. Early in 1968, the Society began to organize one-day conferences to 'train the trainers', as well as programming its central two-day course.

Although some active interest in Sandhurst's innovations in leadership training had been shown already by industrial and public service bodies, it was the energy and enthusiasm of John Garnett and The Industrial Society which really lifted this form of training off the ground and into a wider world. It is interesting to discover not only the kind of organizations which adopted ACL in the following years, but also their reasons for being attracted to it.

In 1969, a pilot survey had involved the sending out of 270 questionnaires to training managers who had attended fourteen one-day Training for Action-Centred Leadership courses. Of the 125 replies received, 59 completed the questionnaires and gave details of the application of ACL. Forty-two delegates replied by letter that they intended to use ACL during the following year, and a further 23 delegates replied negatively. The time elapsing between the courses and the survey was so short that many experienced difficulty in completing the questionnaire.

A survey in 1970, arranged more professionally (by David Charles–Edwards and published by The Industrial Society as *A Report on the Application of Action-Centred Leadership*), was based on much the same-size sample and included many of the 1969 respondents. Of the 126 replies, some 72 organizations were using ACL on an in-company basis, and the other 54 had announced plans to do so in the near future. (By the end of 1972, some 300 organizations in the UK had informed The Industrial Society that they use ACL, and so the reader may care to note that the 1970 Report deals with less than one-third of those now known to be using ACL.) The analysis of the organizations, and their reasons for using ACL as reported in 1970, can be summarized under two main headings :

(a) *Type of Organization.* One striking fact is that all kinds of organizations have adopted ACL training. Industries ranging from manufacturing to retail, banks, insurance companies, local government, public services, the armed services, churches, charities; it would be difficult to find any kind of working body which is not represented. The 1970 Survey illustrated this :

Type of Organization	Already using ACL	Planning to use ACL	Total
Manufacturing—consumer	22	14	36
Manufacturing—industrial	23	24	47
Retail/wholesale	6	4	10
Commercial	5	3	8
Nationalized industries	6	0	6
Government administration	3	2	5
Research and training	5	3	8
Other (including social services)	2	4	6
Total:	72	54	126

Much time is spent, justifiably so, in analysing the precise training needs of a given organization, and managers are more aware today of the unique *personality* of their firm which must be reflected in the training sphere. The strategy which works in one organization may not necessarily work in another, even when they are both in the same industry. But there are also *general* needs, created by the social and technological transformations of the day, which seem to affect a very wide range of organizations, albeit in different forms and degrees of intensity. Such is the need for leadership training.

(b) *Size of Organization.* It could be argued that size (in terms of numbers of employees) does create a special urgency for education and training in 'the human side of enterprise'. It is all too easy for the individual to be lost in the mammoth organizational whale's belly. The challenge of gaining 'economies of size' without sacrificing human values stands high on the list of those who must cope with civilization in the coming decades. General or social philosophy, reflected in structural changes which emphasize small and local groupings, can have long-term effects, but to provide shorter-term encouragements, good leadership is always a necessity.

On the other hand, it has historically been the 'big battalions' that have had the money for training and the specialist staff to do it. By 1968 many medium-sized and smaller companies had recognized the need for training in the broad field of leadership and motivation, and were looking for a method of going about it which could be adapted to the essentially practical backgrounds of their managers and supervisors as well as the size of their budgets. My own experience in 1967 with Wilson (Connolly) Holdings Ltd, a group of small Midlands building firms employing 1200 men, gave me some insight into their particular training problems and opportunities.

By 1970 it was clear that organizations of all sizes, ranging from the Post Office (over 300 000 employees) to small local firms of a score or two people, had shown a positive interest in ACL. The 1970 figures were as follows:

Number of Employees	Already using ACL	Planning to use ACL	Total
0–200	7	6	13
201–1 000	10	7	17
1 001–5 000	26	20	46
5 001–15 000	12	4	16
15 001–30 000	4	3	7
Over 30 000	10	6	16
Not given	3	8	11
Total:	72	54	126

We know that ACL originated as an answer to a training need in a big organization (the British Army). It retains the ability to cope with large numbers in situations where there are few training specialists. It employs the specialists in an advisory role to line managers, who actually lead the ACL conferences as part of their overall responsibility for leadership

73

development. Naturally this is easier to arrange in a training-centred institution like Sandhurst. But the principle can be applied in modified forms in any large organization, by a process of secondment to the training department. On the other hand, taking more time, it is possible to train specialists to lead the courses themselves, and this has been the pattern in many of the organizations, large and small, that have adopted ACL training.

SOME CHARACTERISTICS OF ACL

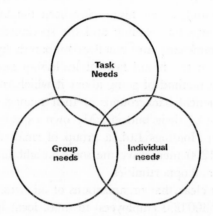

Leadership training based upon the three circle model and the emphasis on *functions* as opposed to qualities made its way from the Armed Services, into industry, commerce and the public services on a world scale, because it possessed certain distinctive characteristics. I invented none of these characteristics or hallmarks myself. I merely recognized them, and have sought to share my enthusiasm for them and conviction that together they give the right direction for this kind of education or training. Thus I feel no inhibitions in writing briefly in praise of them.

Simple. Many have commented on the essential *simplicity* of the three circle model and of ACL generally. 'Simple' is not the same as 'simplistic', 'simpliste' or 'superficial', which imply a fundamental lack of depth or penetration, for true simplicity can also be profound when we think more deeply about it. It can exhibit many levels or facets of meaning to the inquiring mind yet it makes an immediate and satisfying impact on virtually everyone. The *Shorter Oxford English Dictionary* offers

74

three clusters of uses for the word *simple*, all of which I hope apply to ACL:

- Free from duplicity, dissimulation, or guile; innocent and harmless; undesigning, honest, open, straightforward.
- Free from, devoid of, pride, ostentation, or display; humble, unpretentious.
- Free from elaboration or artificiality; artless, unaffected; plain, unadorned.

The author of the 1970 *Survey* reported that 14 organizations had highlighted the value of the three-circles diagram: 'several of them praised its simplicity and freedom from complex jargon; its simplicity and self-evidence give it power'. The discerning reader will also have noticed how often the words *simple* or *simplicity* crop up in the remarks of the contributors to this book. It is always difficult to be simple, but the reward is a much wider communication.

Practical. As the name implies, Action-Centred Leadership keeps its eyes firmly fixed upon the *doing* aspects of leadership rather than the *being* (or qualities) facets of it. 'Good thoughts', wrote Francis Bacon, 'though acceptable to God, yet towards men are little better than good dreams.' Although ACL can claim success in changing attitudes, or mental states, it understands these as essentially the dispositions that lead to action. They are therefore disclosed in activity. Those actions may be dramatic, or they may be decidely unspectacular—a smile of encouragement, a word at the right time. But the emphasis in ACL falls mainly on what has to be done to *lead effectively*. And this stress appeals to the essentially practical and pragmatic minds of managers and supervisors, who are mainly concerned with results and measurable changes in terms of the organization's purpose. Conversely, ACL has less appeal to those who are mainly interested in ideas, the analysis of personality or group processes as ends in themselves.

Participative. The highly participative character of ACL attracts favourable comment. Adults much prefer to learn through discussion and discovery, and the practical element in some of the exercises underlines the central theme of the course. Participation begins always in the very first session, and it sets a standard for the rest of the course. Obviously ACL shares this characteristic with other training approaches, but it seems to stand out in ACL, perhaps as it is a relatively short course.

In writing about the reasons why a large department store (John Lewis of Oxford Street) adopted ACL, Mrs Maureen Pearson has emphasized its teaching methods:

66 Part of our experience as a Training Department had given us dissatisfaction in the traditional talk/chalk training function. If we were to help managers become more skilled, then we had to let them practise these skills. In other words, to talk of leadership and management skills is rather like expecting someone to learn how to drive a car by talking about it and, added to that, the talk will be given by a back seat driver. To learn a skill requires practice.

It had become apparent that retailers need action, if you are to maintain their interest; they are greater doers than thinkers.

ACL seemed to match these needs—long-term development and immediate needs for practising the skills of leadership. Having sampled and assessed a course run by The Industrial Society, we agreed upon its potential usefulness, and the whole of the Training Department then had an appreciation course. **99**

The three hallmarks—*simple*, *practical*, and *participative*—do not exhaust the characteristics of ACL training. For example, it is comparatively *short* and relatively *inexpensive* to adopt (The Industrial Society is a non-profit-making body). Moreover, the potential *comprehensiveness* of ACL is such an important feature that it merits a separate chapter (chapter seven). But the simplicity of its model, ACL's practical orientation and highly participative methods first catch the imagination of possible users. These values become evident when the ACL course is run experimentally on an in-company basis: a method of validation which is worthy of separate consideration because it has played such an important part in the progress of ACL.

In concluding this section, it is worth giving two organizational judgements on ACL training: 'We all know that ACL is not the only factor to be considered,' John Lyons (the Director of Industrial Relations at Caterpillar Tractor) has written, 'and that in a constantly dynamic situation, many factors affect results for better or worse. Nevertheless, we feel confident that we will reap both tangible and intangible rewards from ACL which is in our view the most comprehensive yet simple, practical and work-related development programme we have encountered to date.'

In a work sphere far removed from that of Caterpillar Tractor the training staff of the Post Office Supervisory Training Centre have echoed this judgement : 'The ACL concept first aroused our interest because of its diagramatic simplicity, the participative approach and the way in which the basic principles of management are portrayed. It seemed to us that for the first time many of the theories and ideas about Man Management, Leadership, Motivation, and Group Dynamics could be knitted together and illustrated simply and in a practical form using the ACL concept as a vehicle.' We shall look at this latter possibility in the following chapter; it is sufficient here to note how both organizations discerned the essential hallmarks or characteristics of ACL training.

TRAINING NEEDS AND TRIAL RUNS

The statistics suggest that a wide range of organizations in terms of type and size have found ACL relevant to their training needs. In the progress of ACL much has depended upon the awareness and identification of this underlying need for leadership training, for that is logically prior to the adoption of any one approach. What has happened in many cases is the dawn of an understanding that there is now an essential training need to develop leadership (or a management which encompasses the human resources as well as the material ones) coupled with the intuition that ACL, because of its special characteristics, might be able to meet that need.

This mental state has to be turned into a discovery by some sort of experience. Even though the training specialist may have become convinced himself, perhaps by participating in a nationally organized course or by sitting in and observing on someone else's course, he has yet to convince himself and his colleagues that the ACL approach will work in his own company, with its unique ethos or personality. Thus a frequent 'next step' is to organize one or more trial runs, which are strictly experimental and designed both to evaluate the training at first hand, so to speak, and to uncover the adaptations that the particular organizational situation dictates. The National Coal Board, for example, ran seven pilot courses in the Doncaster area training centre before launching into a programme involving more than 2000 managers and supervisors.

Such pilot schemes are especially important where large numbers are involved. The Postal Business (that section of the Post Office which excludes Telecommunications) employs more than 170 000 people of whom over 13 000 are supervisors. During the last year or so the Personnel Division (Training) has reviewed supervisory training with the objective of improving supervisory performance particularly in the leadership/management fields.

“We held a controlled series of two-day trials with students being selected on random basis and being representative of all shades of supervision. These trials were closely monitored and the students were aware of the purpose of the experiment, which was to evaluate this approach. The trials proved successful in that students were able to grasp the principles quickly, their interest was aroused and they enjoyed the experience. Perhaps what is more important, follow-up evaluation indicated that they had—with some limitations, been able to make the transition from the training situation to the work place.”

Caterpillar Tractor involved different levels of management from the start, as Jack Frost, Education and Training Manager at the Glasgow Plant, writes:

“We decided to expose our Management to the training down the organization structure in a horizontal slice, and that the first three meetings, one of senior Managers and two of Middle Managers, should be conducted by a tutor from The Industrial Society. We followed these with one meeting of General Foremen and then composite groups of factory and office supervisors. We ensured that each group of approximately 20 conferees contained a good mix of factory and office. These sessions were conducted by our own Training Division team.”

This experimental or 'trial' approach should never be abandoned, even when ACL has become an accepted part of the total educational and training programme. Again the Postal Business example illustrates this continuing process of modification and improvement:

“Apart from gaining information about the effective application of training we also use evaluation to assess particular material and sessions. We review sessions which consistently get a low rating, and we make sure that more time is given to those in which the students and the Postal Business have indicated a deficiency in knowledge and skills. In addition, the post-exercise discussions were analysed in terms of relevant and irrelevant remarks. The analysis illustrated the progressive appreciation of the objectives of the course by the students.”

A list of some of the organizations which have gone through this process and adopted ACL is given in the Appendix. This list is not complete as hundreds of other companies include substantial elements of ACL in training programmes, and over 2500 organizations have sent delegates

78

to Industrial Society courses. But it will give the reader a representative cross-section of the kinds of organizations who have found ACL useful. Incidentally, it was (and is) a part of the conditions under which ACL is made available that organizations should be willing to be approached by inquirers for their judgements on ACL. This process of inquiry is illustrated by the experience of Reed International Ltd :

66 The first formal contact between Reed personnel and ACL was at an Industrial Society Leadership Workshop session in May 1970. Following this, W. D. Gabbitus, Director of Central Management Courses, and A. H. Extance, Supervisory Training Adviser, set out to find out more about the effectiveness of ACL. At the same time, an associate company, Kimberly-Clark Ltd, became interested in ACL and their Management Development and Training Officer A. W. Harvey, with A. H. Extance, arranged a visit to Thanet Press, Margate, to discuss with the training officer their experience with ACL. As a result of this visit :

- Reed International incorporated two ACL exercises into existing Human Relations training sessions in a current Supervisor Course. The objective was to test supervisors' reactions to the type of exercises that were a feature of ACL, and to get the 'feel' of the approach. The results of these experiments were encouraging, and the potential of the ACL approach to training in the Human Relations area began to be appreciated.

- Kimberly-Clark made further contact with The Industrial Society and, following a half-day orientation session, engaged a Society tutor to present a two-day course (with A. H. Extance 'understudying'), followed by further courses conducted by Mr Extance and Kimberly-Clark staff.

These experiences satisfied Reed International as to the potential of ACL as a training tool.**99**

It was, and is, a part of the agreement between users of ACL and The Industrial Society that organizations share their experience, lessons, and improvements with each other and the Society. These two factors have undoubtedly accelerated the speed with which ACL has spread in the United Kingdom and abroad.

ACL IN DIFFERENT CULTURES

One test of any form of training is how culturally determined it is. Cultural, social, or implicit philosophical assumptions are rather like germs: invisible and easily carried by bearers who are unaware of their presence. For this reason a careful combination of trial runs is important when transposing a form of training from one cultural climate to another. If such training does not accord with the deeper values of the culture it may be enthusiastically received for a while and spring up all over the place, but eventually it will wither away and die. In doing so it may modify the culture, but the merits of that process in itself should rest on a value judgement which in practice is not always consciously made.

Fortunately, good leadership is a natural phenomena, easily recognizable in any culture or continent. It is in the secondary writings about leadership, especially those which touch on the so-called 'styles of leadership', that cultural distortions may enter. The situational approach to the sharing of decisions between leader and team or group members allows for the cultural factor (along with others) to be taken into consideration in determining the appropriate point on the continuum at a given time. ACL has safeguarded itself against being tied to one set of assumptions or value judgements which would have anchored it firmly to one culture, if not even more closely to a sub-culture.

Confirmation of this freedom has come from the extension of ACL throughout the world. Australia has seen some successful ACL courses. In November 1971 the Queensland Division of The Australian Institute of Management reported:

“To date, we have conducted eight Courses/Laboratories/Workshops, based purely on the Action-Centred Leadership concept. In addition to this, the concept has formed a part of other Courses, ranging from Supervisor training to Executive Development training—about a further 20 activities in all. The concept has been enthusiastically received by delegates to all Courses. These delegates would come from many levels of management, as well as specialist organizations such as the Police, the Queensland Ambulance Brigade and Youth Organizations. In all, some five hundred people have trained in Action-Centred Leadership.”

It may be argued that Australia and New Zealand stand close to the British culture, as does Norway for that matter (whose army showed a keen early interest in Functional Leadership training). But ACL in part or whole has also been introduced effectively into India, Malaya, Ethiopia, Uganda, Saudi Arabia, Belgium, Venezuela, Pakistan, and the United State. There is mounting evidence, even in these early days, that its sim-

80

plicity, practicality, and participative methods attract universal interest. But then good leadership is a universal fact and necessity.

FOUR CASE HISTORIES

Four case histories (from the Coal Industry, the Fire Service, Local Government, and Industry) are presented to illustrate the themes of this chapter. In particular they evoke those technological and social changes which have done so much to create the awareness of a definite training need for leadership. Besides this common denominator, some of them describe the way in which the organizations concerned came across ACL training or subjected it to their own tests. They substantiate the bare facts and figures of the progress of ACL since 1968 by giving some of the background thinking which went into the decision to adopt and adapt ACL in four particular organizations.

The National Coal Board. In the British coal industry the conditions creating the need for leadership training came from the interplay of internal technological factors and the decline in the size of the industry. In the decade 1960–1970 the large rise in output per man-year (305 to 463 tons) was mainly due to the spread of power loading, which extends the mechanization of the movement of coal from the coal-face. But, for national reasons, the manpower declined from 602 000 to 287 000 (largely by 'natural wastage'). In 1966 the National Coal Board and National Union of Mineworkers agreed to replace piece rates with day rates. Inevitably, this created human problems. Edwin Hutchinson, who was responsible for an ACL programme involving more than 2000 first-line managers and supervisors in the Doncaster area (the largest of the NCB's 17 areas), describes how these problems were especially marked for the district deputies (first-line management):

66 Traditionally, coal had been worked by men 'contracting' to their employer on a local basis to carry out certain operations for a certain wage. This wage was based on a sliding scale so that, broadly speaking, the more effective work a man produced the more money he was paid. The men worked basically in sections spaced out along the coal-face either filling coal on to a conveyor or building roof supports out of stone, wood or steel. Only in the case of roadway drivage (at the extreme ends of the face) did more than two men work together. In such instances the teams were still small: generally not more than

81

three or four men. The work was of a heavy manual nature, involving the use of handtools, shovels, hammers, and picks, and the amount of work a man 'contracted' to carry out depended upon his own particular mining skills, physical condition, and financial goals.

These teams of face men were supervised by a member of first-line management called a District Deputy. His basic role was to carry out the requirements of Coal Mining Legislation having regard for the safety of the men under his control, and to make sure that the financial goals of operations did not conflict with safe working methods. He was also charged by management with checking, by measurements, the amount of work produced by each man and with agreeing with these men any additional payments due to them for dealing with abnormalities outside the terms of the negotiated contracts. In summarizing his role it might be said that he 'supervised' his men with safety and contract payments uppermost in mind. Generally speaking this level of management was drawn from the ranks of first-class workmen, who had qualified as District Deputies in their youth, but had reached the age where physically they were not capable of meeting the demands of the contractual system any longer.

Mechanization meant that men began to work as groups or teams of five or six, following the machines as they passed along the coal-face cutting and loading coal. As these machines proved successful coal-faces began to be worked on multiple shifts. The increased rate of production meant that roadways had to be advanced more rapidly within the shift and the three- or four-man teams were expanded to cope with increased work up to the present levels of five and six men.

Changes in mechanization and systems of payment dramatically affected the first-line supervisory role. The technology of machine mining now required men to work in groups of five or six. Payment by the daywage system discouraged men from seeking out clear definitions of their shift tasks. Obviously, the more successful supervisors would be those who could adopt a style which concentrated on satisfying the task and group needs of the team.

There were clear indications that much of the work the District Deputy had done so successfully before in satisfying individual needs had now to some extent been superseded by the participative practices of worker involvement that had become commonplace. He had clearly not understood his new *leading* role, had not moved his operations into the task and group circle, had not seized opportunities in meeting individual needs of the groups in their changed circumstances. He had turned his attention towards managing the machinery and saw the problems of man management as of secondary importance. He had become a *controller of operations* rather than a leader of a team of men.

Experience of worker involvement had made management realize that strict management controls used on single-shift mechanized coalfaces could not survive in the multi-shift environment, if conflict between teams of men was to be avoided. Old-style supervision had been eroded away by the elimination of the stick-and-carrot contractual system, and the controlling style of management would not survive the attacks that worker participation and involvement methods were making upon it. As the under-officials struggled with various degrees of success to retain control at the collieries, it was interesting to see the way in which this vacuum of control was enthusiastically filled by the miners, when management had had sufficient foresight to create a climate conducive to involvement practices.

The culmination of research into the under-official's question, 'What is my role now?' was the realization that worker involvement presupposes a movement of decision-making power from managerial level down to the shop floor; in our case to the coal-face.

Careful consideration led us to recognize that the under-official's new role should be that of leader. Leading his team towards more control of their working environment; leading them to arrive at the best possible decisions; fulfilling the essential link in two-way communications between management and worker which is so necessary for total involvement. His greatest challenge would be managing the ever-changing needs of the task, and satisfying group and individual needs of the teams, which new technologies had created.

After some investigation, it was decided to run a number of two-day pilot ACL courses. Two training instructors attended a one-day tutors' course, and subsequently ran seven courses at the area training centre.

This somewhat cautious beginning was interrupted in October 1969 by a strike, on a national question, which immobilized collieries and left us with a number of under-employed officials. We took the opportunity to run a series of ACL courses at colliery level. This brought our course coverage up to 400 under-officials.

In the aftermath of the strike, courses were suspended, and in late December we began to evaluate course impact. The evaluation system used was simple:

- What have you remembered about leadership?
- What effect, if any, has the course had upon relationships between men and management and across levels of management?

The results of the survey proved that this course was significantly more successful in terms of knowledge retention and possible practical application than any similar course we had run.

Armed with this knowledge the Area Executive Committee decided that during 1970 all under-officials should attend a similar two-day Leadership course, and it was also realized that there was a real need to run ACL courses for middle and senior management grades.**

The Manchester Fire Service. The Manchester Fire Service adopted Functional Leadership training directly from Sandhurst in 1967. The Chief Officer, Mr H. Lomas CBE, describes the effects of the changing social climate on an organization impregnated with traditional ways of thinking about leadership:

**Traditionally, the Service had developed an authoritarian type of leadership which had served a useful purpose. The erosion of this type of leadership grew as the men became better organized and challenged attempts to rule by decree. Unfortunately, the Service was at a loss how to re-shape its attitudes and many delicate and dangerous situations arose.

The leader concept began to figure more prominently, and fortuitously it fitted neatly into the operational pattern. Fire crews function under great stress and are conditioned to work at full stretch in any emergency situation. Under these conditions, the common task is usually accomplished to the satisfaction of the team. Success is shared, as is failure, and the team is conscious of the need to maintain itself as a cohesive force for its own protection when actively engaged on the ground. The Service finds that the leadership function works extremely well in operational situations no matter how stressful but it experiences increasing difficulties in getting things done under normal or routine circumstances.

Functional leadership training identified some of the difficulties without solving all the problems. There is at least a clear understanding why a busy operational fire station achieves and maintains a higher level of morale and efficiency than does the quiet station with little operational movement. The understanding and interpretation of these facts has helped to inject more purpose into the routine working of stations.

The two principal fire service objectives (to save life from fire, and to prevent the destruction of property) are well understood by its members. When not actively in pursuit of them, the Service feels a sense of frustration and lack of purpose. The Service is not entirely clear what is meant by Management by Objectives. It considers that there are no effective means of quantifying results, no means of setting targets and measuring achievements; it develops a feeling and attitude that because there is no beginning there cannot be an end.

Because of increasing frustration, grave problems have bedevilled the Service; men are not unmindful of increasing militancy in industry; resistance to unpopular shift and weekend working, generally unfavourable attitudes to discipline and indifferent recruitment, have, in their own way, affected the traditional officer/man relationships. The difficulties in maintaining a highly mobile force properly motivated and conscious of the quality of the service it renders to the community have been great.

Top management has now recognized its changing role. In recent years there has been increasing reluctance to resort to the Discipline Code, and an urge to move into closer contact with the ground (shop floor). Shortcomings have been noted and examined with a desire to improve personal performance. Functional Leadership training can claim much of the credit.**"**

Local Government. The changing scene in local government and the training needs which emerged—needs which ACL could satisfy—are described here by Douglas Tamblin, Training Officer of the London Borough of Hillingdon :

" Most countries have evolved a system of government catering at lower levels for basic and local needs and at higher levels for more remote and complex needs. Local problems should be solved at local levels; as they move away from their source they become more difficult and more costly to solve. If *local* government, through improved organization, is able to tackle more effectively the nation's business it would reduce workloads in *central* government. To this end, in the United Kingdom, Royal Commissions were set up to improve the functioning of local government, culminating in the Redcliffe–Maud proposals for a major reorganization in 1975.

In London reorganization followed the Local Government Act of 1963, and by 1965 the two-tier system consisted of a Greater London Council and 32 chartered boroughs. This shake-up had many repercussions, one of which was the development of management services, as boroughs settled down to their new responsibilities. In 1968 in company with other training officers in the London area, I set about the task of staff training.

The inertia of local government made the going difficult. Hillingdon, like most other boroughs, exhibited symptoms of organizational rundown. There was over-stability in the upper levels and high turnover at operator level, particularly among manual employees. There was little cohesion among the separate departments, and much conflict between staff and line functions. In such circumstances, entrenchment had resulted in a blurring of the task and, with the absence of well-defined work objectives, other objectives had taken their place to dissipate individual effort. De-motivation had resulted in many cases, and of course this lowers performance and destroys any incentive to plan for the future, to anticipate crisis, or to improve the organization.

In such circumstances, the problems are so interrelated that it is hard to know where to start unravelling them. To improve one part of an organization, other parts have to be improved, it being difficult to identfy cause and effect. To make matters worse, new people were introduced into the boroughs with the aim of improving organization and methods, and to introduce work study based incentive schemes. Fears were thus injected into the situation : fear of loss of jobs, skills, earnings, status, companions, surroundings, and also of the capacity to cope with change. There was an even more complex problem : the substitution of management jargon for the real disciplines of systematic organization and control.

Perhaps these facts appear irrelevant, but they need to be appreciated if the reader is to understand how ACL solved *our particular* training problem.

The name Action-Centred Leadership may, at first, have given the wrong impression, because 'leadership' is a word not often used in local government. However, it is spreading quickly, and Hillingdon's training is firmly rooted in ACL; it forms the central concept, the basis on which our training is built. It is with personal conviction that I present to any trainer the concept of ACL as a practical tool which is capable of bringing an organization to life, and motivating its members.**"**

At this point, Mr Tamblin described the administrative burden imposed on a training officer in Local Government. With a total of 511 types of job—from abattoir workers to zoo keepers—it was hard to identify all the training needs, and so it became necessary to single out first the key or strategic training needs.

66 There were three stages: first, the training need was identified, then it was discovered that a simple and obvious concept appeared to meet the need, and third, a demonstration showed how the concept could be adapted to a classroom situation.

The need was identified by our Director of Management Services, who said: 'There's an awful lot of useless management training. The problem is to get people to do things to help the system along without being told to do so. That wastepaper basket, now, is full but who will notice it and bother to empty it?' In essence this is the problem—achieving results through others: making members of an organization think and do instead of merely going through the minimal motions to keep out of trouble. The supervisor who can so motivate her typists that they empty their wastepaper baskets unasked is valuable because many other 'extras' will be done unasked.

The supervisor may have laid down good work routines, but without the compelling force which makes a typist follow those routines they may as well not exist. This motivation will occur only if typists feel so identified with the corporate task that they are compelled to help in every way they can to achieve the aims of their group.

When I first learned of Action-Centred Leadership, the simple *concept* of Task, Team, and Individual Needs immediately appealed. In theory the concept (see Fig 1.1) clarified my own nebulous ideas and enabled me critically to examine the results of group dynamics training courses that some of our staff were attending at the time. As far as I could judge, there was little emphasis in such training on the task to be performed, and without a task there can be no purposeful activity.

I was more convinced that the *simple* ACL concept was the answer to my problems when I considered it in the context of some research I had undertaken some ten years before. I used matrix analysis, a technique developed by the Royal Air Force to help in linear programmes. I wanted to find out what had gone wrong with the teaching of mathematics. Among many other things I found that the closer to reality and the simpler the operations, the more powerful mathematics became as an instrument of progress. Milestones in the history of mathematics were *simple* effective answers to pressing human needs. The cipher zero, the negative number, the ratio and binary arithmetic were the 'obvious' answers to the needs of the time but each brought in its wake great progress. Action-Centred Leadership could prove the *simple* and *obvious* answer to the effective use of manpower and, in particular, the public servant.

I first saw leadership training demonstrated in a seminar run by The Industrial Society for clerical supervisors. It made a great impact on course members, and there was obviously a lift in performance afterwards. Attitudes to work improved and in particular the traditional complaint of 'too much work and too few staff' was heard less often. Since this course in mid-1969 leadership training has been an essential element in all supervisory, management, and development courses in my Local Authority. The methods of presentation vary with the level of the course but the principles appeal to all. The reasons for this appeal vary with the individual but because it is a conceptual approach it is a good communicator. The principles are realistic enough to be demonstrated in simulated work situations in which individual performance can be measured against performance required to reach defined objectives. Training can thus be validated on the spot.

Most people find that Functional Leadership is a realistic model of the work situation. There are few natural leaders, but many who possess a certain degree of leadership potential and these can be helped to improve their performance by clear and convincing presentation in training situations.

It is gratifying that many line managers who are trained in leadership realize (and usually quite suddenly) that 'authority' expects them to lead. This knowledge is a strong motivation; it gives status, and allies the leader to the task and the objectives of the organization. Once motivation of the supervisor or manager is achieved, there is a strong urge towards task achievment, and a desire to clear away obstacles in the way of achievement. It is then that the manager begins to review everything he must do to achieve his objectives.

Training becomes a 'blanket' if the training *needs* are not precisely identified for each person in each job. A training need is nothing more than the difference between a man's actual performance and the performance required by the job. The organization's responsibility to the line manager is to see that he is given a system of staff performance appraisal, and has a task analysis of each job performed by his subordinates. In my Authority, Management by Objectives is defining present and required performance at top management levels (on average some 15 per department) and Work Measurement at the operator level. This focus of attention on his working group clarifies the role of the line manager; gives him the status to represent his group to the other parts of the organization; involves and develops his subordinates in the interests of the organization; objectifies and lifts performance continually.

Many early attempts to reorganize local government internally, and to introduce training or incentive schemes, failed to take into account the key role played by line managers. Not only was the line manager torn between earning bonus and maintaining his work team, catering for individual needs and training his staff, but his take-home pay was very frequently less than some of his work team. This increased tension at the most critical points in the organization. One of the first effects of leadership training with supervisors was a realization that incentive bonus schemes must be redesigned to reinforce the proper function of all management levels—particularly first liners.**

Vauxhall Motors. The importance of identifying training needs and evaluating ACL in the light of them is emphasized by this contribution from C. J. Hayes of Vauxhall Motors. He also stresses the practical or pragmatic dimension of ACL which fitted in with the ethos of his firm. In addition Vauxhall evolved their own model (see page 90) based on the three circles, suggestive of the possibilities of ACL as an integrating concept:

**The introduction at Vauxhall of a Management Manpower Audit system of management staff appraisal, brought, among other benefits, a more specific and concentrated recognition of training needs in management personnel. Not only was there an awareness of an overall shortage of adequate training, but individual needs of managers and supervisors were identified much more readily. Among these were human relations, communications (written and oral), and decision-making.

It was found that an area in which management could benefit most from greater knowledge was that of understanding the problems involved in leading people and in knowing the people themselves. Many clerks, draughtsmen, and engineers had achieved promotion to supervisory positions without formalized training on the main aspect of a job which was totally new to them—managing the work of others.

89

The situation with factory-floor based operations, that is for foremen, was somewhat better.

The need for additional management training was evident at more than one level, and a decision had to be taken on where to start. It was eventually decided that the most critical stratum occurred between second-line supervision (general foremen, senior engineers, systems analysts, etc) and executives with responsibility for whole divisions (production area managers, sales managers, finance managers, etc). In the event, although it was not envisaged at the outset, there has been a tendency to concentrate on newly-appointed personnel.

Management at Vauxhall has always had a strongly pragmatic content. Thus any training programme had to offer more than an introduction to the theories of certain behavioural scientists or an apprecia-

tion of the skills of communication. The overriding need, and the only way of ensuring acceptance, was to make certain that trainees could see the applicability of the concepts in their own environments.

This necessitated the development of a programme which had to meet the following requirements:

● It must teach the concepts of leadership, need-satisfaction, group dynamics, motivation.

90

- It must show, through practical exercises, that the concepts are true and do work (experiential learning).
- It must physically be related to participant's work situations.
- It must show where the concepts contribute to the functions and responsibilities of management and how they affect aspects of managerial activity.

In order to achieve the last two of these objectives it was necessary to develop an in-plant programme. Vauxhall had the facilities and the staff and so the need was to establish a conceptual basis for the programme. After some deliberation it was decided that it should be developed around the three-circles concept of the 'Action-Centred Leadership' Programme.

This concept, propagating as it does the idea that what is important is what a leader *does* to lead effectively, not simply what he *is* or *knows*, was likely to have maximum appeal to the down-to-earth manager at Vauxhall.

As the course emerged, so did the desirability of establishing a model of management to serve the dual purpose of :

- Establishing in participants' minds an overall understanding of what management is all about, and
- sub-dividing this overall understanding into four areas for administrative purposes (e.g., filing and indexing).

The three circles form the central features of the model. This is no accident—nor is it to enhance the graphic appeal of the model! It simply reflects the importance of the circles in the sum total of management.**"**

The objective of this chapter has been to give the reader some further insights into *why* such a range of organizations, in many different fields and of many shapes and sizes, have taken up ACL training. Some general factors and tendencies may be discerned : technological and social changes, the mushroom growth of management education and training, and the economic pressures towards better performance. These factors, working together, created (and are creating) an unprecedented need for leadership, a demand which far outstrips the natural supply of 'born leaders'. By the middle of the last decade ACL had already proved itself to be effective and acceptable to both the course participants and senior management as a method for exploring the nature of leadership and arriving at action programmes for leaders in given situations.

5. Getting the best results from ACL

Getting the best results from ACL

Naturally, organizations or individuals using ACL want to get the best results from it, just as a musician hopes to conjure the finest tunes from a given instrument. This analogy reminds us that there is no substitute for the trainer's own professional competence. Given this, it should not be difficult for him or her to grasp the essentials of ACL's contents and methods. This can be best done through the natural processes of observation, apprenticeship, a trial run (with feedback from an experienced person), and then learning through the trial-and-error process. Fortunately ACL is robust, and it can still be effective if the trainer is not highly skilled in the relevant arts in the early stages of his own training as a tutor.

But general and specialized ability on the part of the trainer is not the whole answer. Inevitably ways of improving the 'yield per acre' of ACL have been canvassed in the past three or four years, not least by the author. Some of these possibilities have been tried; others await the bold innovator. The objective of this chapter is to look at four 'debates' about getting the best results from ACL. The reader will note that they are not all of the same importance, but no matter—for all the topics have occurred frequently in questions or discussions. My object is not to close these debates but to present some of the arguments and practical experience which will lead the reader to make his own informed judgements. As to the order of the following sections, I have followed the sequence of before, during and after the course, although the training department would in fact make decisions about all these 'debates' long before the course was held.

HOW MANY PARTICIPANTS?

People often ask whether or not better results would be obtained if the size of the course was kept small. Originally ACL was based on a group of about 20 members under one tutor or trainer, working in a rhythm of plenary and small group meetings (four syndicates of five) on discussion questions and observation exercises over a two-day period. This combination promised the best results in the given situation at Sandhurst, and has proved widely acceptable in other organizations.

The underlying principle is that the numbers should be small enough to permit a high degree of individual participation and large enough to allow a fruitful exchange of ideas and experience. For a three-day (or less) course, this principle, if applied, would set limits of not less than 12 and not more than 24 members. My own preference is for 15, 18 or 20, which divide conveniently into three syndicates of 5 or 6, or four of 5 members.

To discover what was happening in practice, the author of the 1970 Report asked organizations to give the average number of delegates per course. Bearing in mind non-training considerations, such as the availability of managers, the average number is likely to represent the opinion of the organization of what is the best and most viable number for a course in practice. In fact, smaller groups dominate: two-thirds kept them to 15 or below; only one-sixth ran courses of 20 or above. These figures may be influenced (it must be said again) partly by the difficulty sometimes of collecting together a larger number for in-company training at the same time.

The actual breakdown was as follows:

Average number of delegates per course								
7–9	10-11	12–13	14–15	16–17	18–19	20–21	22-24	Total
Number of Organizations								
3	7	21	13	3	8	7	3	65

These figures are not correlated with the length of the course, but I suspect that the longer a course the more participants should be involved in order to make possible the freshness of the dialogue of experience right up to the last hour. Conversely, the shorter the course programme the less people it can accommodate, unless more than one tutor is employed. All these considerations may seem common sense, and so they are, but they are often neglected.

ONE OR MORE LEVELS?

A main argument against involving two levels of management in ACL courses is the danger of possible conflicts between the two role-sets of 'fellow students' and 'boss-and-subordinate'. It would not be easy to keep these separate : for instance, for a subordinate to comment in public on the leadership performance of his boss in an exercise, or for the latter to avoid taking mental notes on his junior to be used in evidence at some future appraisal interview. The aim of ACL is to build up relationships in a constructive manner, and not to break them down, either deliberately or heedlessly. Thus, there is a strong case for avoiding these risks by sticking to one level of management on any course. One chief argument for mixing levels on ACL is that it effectively counters the traditional rejoinder : 'You should have sent my boss on this course.' It may also help to bridge the gap between the generations in an organization by creating an informal atmosphere away from the job, where searching conversations can take place. How far training in general should compensate for lack of such opportunities in the working situation is, however, a discussion point in itself.

There is an obvious compromise solution : to mix levels but without including those who directly work with each other. This method retains the richer mixture of ideas and experience contributed by the presence of different levels, but it does not facilitate more effective application of ACL in a department or section as much as the more risky two-level course involving an actual pair or team of managers who must then apply the training together in their work situation.

In the 1970 Survey, the 61 respondent organizations who between them had run courses involving 5094 employees, ranging from managing directors to senior technicians, scientists, office section leaders, and charge-hands, were divided on the advisability of mixing levels. Of 58 who answered the question, 31 did mix and 27 did not. Some of the former specified that the mixing should be *diagonal* to avoid a subordinate and boss on the same course. Two, however, had used the whole management team of a smaller factory on one course. In another company, management trainees attend the supervisors' course.

Many organizations have seized on the value of including as wide a spectrum of line and staff management responsibility in the one-level type of course. Thus, variety can be introduced without mixing levels. In this way ACL can contribute to the easing of some of the 'team maintenance' tensions, such as beset any large enterprise. Richard Matanle, Regions Director of Oxfam, noted this important effect :

❝ The first course was run for Divisional and Area Directors and was led by a member of The Industrial Society staff at Oxfam HQ.

97

It immediately became clear that, within the ACL concept, there lay a solution to a number of problems. As one by-product, the fact that the courses were arranged so that those attending were divided equally between Oxfam House staff and regional staff, began to break down the 'We and They' syndrome. The in-house courses have since been repeated to include middle and junior executives and regional organizers on a 50/50 basis.

Without question, the most remarkable effect has been on the total regional structure. The role of the Area Directors has become much more effective. In regular monthly meetings with the Regions Director they have developed a strong sense of objectivity. This has led to the formulation of a three-year Development Plan. The details of this plan, as with the annual budgets, have been worked out by consultation with the regional organizers.**

Other companies, while starting from the author's cautious standpoint in favour of a single broad level, have conducted their own two-level experiments where local circumstances favoured them. Trevor Johnson (a Training Officer in British Insulated Callender's Cables Ltd) describes one such experiment :

**In January 1970, I attended a one-day appreciation of the ACL course, run by The Industrial Society. I was immediately impressed with the 'functional' approach and arranged to attend a two-day course so that I could see how tutors approached the exercises. In addition to appreciating the practical approach, I was impressed by the enjoyment shown by course members. Two months later we ran the first course in BICC. It was highly successful and future courses were quickly booked up. Superintendents (second and third levels of supervisors and their equivalent ranks in non-production areas were the first group to receive this training which, by the end of 1970, was extended to foremen and managers. The courses were run at these three different levels :

- to avoid possible inhibitions;
- to avoid possible exposure of weaknesses to subordinates/superiors;
- to keep the level of discussion and participation at a reasonably similar standard in any group.

One division specifically requested courses in which managers and supervisors would be mixed, and it was found not to have an inhibiting effect on the groups concerned. All knew each other, however, which is not the case in company-wide courses, where the course for foremen is run over three days at the Group Training Centre, and residentially for three days for managers, superintendents, and their equivalents.**

It will be interesting to see whether or not mixed-level training (not just ACL) becomes more widespread. Personally, having tried all the approaches, I prefer the broad but varied single level of management membership, except where special circumstances dictate otherwise.

WHERE SHOULD ACL TRAINING TAKE PLACE?

The environment in which any communication takes place makes its own contribution for good or ill. We all know the problems of thinking or reading in an office connected by the telephone and invaded by callers. On the other hand residential accommodation is expensive, and travel can add to the total bill of time and money. Most large organizations have solved this particular problem by acquiring their own training centre near the strategic crossroads of their divisions. Others prefer hotels or conference centres.

Certainly hotels can help to create a friendly and informal atmosphere. Caterpillar Tractor in Glasgow have run the course over a weekend, on a voluntary basis (this aspect not being common in other companies):

We found that the idea of a preliminary Friday afternoon meeting introduced by the plant manager, followed by a tutor setting the scene for the weekend, was well worth the time and effort needed to 'break the ice' and to demonstrate the commitment of top management to the programme. The weekend was attended voluntarily by the conferees, the Company paying expenses only, and I am convinced that voluntary involvement in the course greatly assists in its acceptance. The 'in-plant' session on the following Monday gave those who had attended the conference the opportunity of discussing it with Senior Management who had themselves previously attended the programme, and also to relate the weekend's teachings to their own work situation.

Usually, however, ACL training takes place in the firm's time and in a suitable setting, which more often than not is residential. Originally the film *Twelve O'Clock High* was shown before and after supper on the first day of the course; indeed, one of the advantages of films is that they offer a change of pace which is most suitable for residential courses,

99

especially if the film concerned has intrinsic entertainment as well as training value.

These points are illustrated by the experience of British Insulated Callender's Cables, who have employed ACL training on a large scale :

66 We find that running the courses residentially is favoured by the majority of trainees for various reasons.

- freedom from work distractions,
- a quickly created social atmosphere,
- extra time for extending discussions and exercises,
- opportunities for making useful contacts,
- a relaxed atmosphere which produces willing participation in trainees, who also
- are able to appreciate colleagues' problems through exchange of ideas and opinions.

Courses start at 3.30 p.m. on Tuesday, allowing at least one day of the week at work) with an introduction to the objectives of the course. Each participant then introduces himself. After dinner *Tunes of Glory* is shown—a film which is both entertaining and thought-provoking. Half-way through we have a brief discussion on 'What are the leader's problems and what is he trying to do?' We have found that it makes an ideal introduction to both basic psychology and leadership and provides a stimulating start to the course.99

INDUSTRY-RELATED EXERCISES?

At first sight it looks as if users of ACL would get better results if they substituted their own industry-related exercises for those practical tasks recommended in the Tutor's Manual. But the difficulty of introducing such 'relevant' tasks is that the observers tend to stop watching the *leadership* aspects of what is happening and to start studying the *technical* pros and cons. It is actually an advantage, in the early stages of a course, if the exercises are *not* drawn from the everyday working environment.

Experience of ACL trainers in a wide range of organizations has confirmed this. Edwin Hutchinson of the National Coal Board, for example, writes :

66 Our reaction initially was to change the Mast Contract practical exercise away from its construction element into one which embraced our own technology of mining. Unfortunately, our substitute exercise

100

provoked technological arguments rather than leadership discussion and therefore did not serve the purpose of the course. Feedback indicates that our decision to revert to the Mast Contract exercise, with all its apparent shortcomings, has proved correct.

Indeed, the Mast Contract exercise has proved interesting in that it is in effect an exercise in involvement something akin to our Coal-face Review Committee meetings. Most teams who take part have the usual problems one would anticipate :

- Conflict between our appointed leader and the group's natural leader;
- Problems of people 'opting' out—non-participants;
- Everyone has a plan—*his* plan.

Most teams do manage eventually to agree on a plan of action and agree objectives in terms of height of tower, number of bricks, and time to build. Most, however, fail to achieve these objectives and fewer still ever feel it necessary to evaluate why the plan failed.**"**

The early non-technological practical exercises in ACL do emphasize the central aim—improving the ability to *observe* leaders and groups at work—as a practical first step towards developing the necessary awareness, understanding, and skill. The Mast Contract, however, is a bit closer to the concerns of industry and commerce because it includes the dimensions of profit and costs. Towards the end of the course the Case Study ('Exercise Remake', Chemical Concentrates, and their variants) should focus everyone's attention on the particular organization, thereby integrating the leadership (or human) and technical aspects of the manager's work. But the stage of separating the former, and considering it in detail first, should not be omitted for the sake of a false instant relevance.

In fact, if one can delay the sudden spark or slow dawn of relevance in the practical work it does no harm, provided the overall course theme and approach is seen to be directly and personally relevant from the start. We are all prepared to suspend judgement for a time, like children listening to a story, if a tutor has established sufficient trust. The more apparently unrelated the practical exercises or films are, the more creative can be the spark which jumps across and lights them with the significance of meaning.

But our personal 'spans of relevance' differ in width. Creative minds can bridge wide gaps and see relationships or patterns in the apparently unrelated or chaotic. Many more, however, can bridge the lesser gap and accept that what is happening in a different organization or industry might be relevant to them. Generally speaking, the higher the level of management the wider should be the span of relevance (especially as organizational problems become more general the more senior one becomes).

As a corollary, the lower the level of management the more it may be necessary to cater for a reduced span of relevance, and supplement ACL with industry-related practical exercises, so that a mix is achieved. With very young management trainees, in a chain of retail stores, for example, I made use of a shop-window changing exercise, using a full-sized version complete with clothes and furniture. At supervisor level the Post Office have also introduced industry-related exercises:

"As a first step we supplemented the leadership exercises with some of our own so that we had a fine mix of Post Office and non-Post Office situations. This was designed to illustrate relevance and to ease the problem of re-entry into the work situation.**"**

In such cases it is important for the tutor to stress continually (by word and example) the leadership observation aspect. The merit of the industry-related dimension at this level of management is that it helps to allay or reduce the nagging sense of 'irrelevance' which may (like one of Herzberg's 'hygiene' factors) mar a foreman's or supervisor's full participation in the course.

These considerations underline the importance of the tutor's role in these practical observation exercises. John Fry of Abbey National Building Society, for example, mentions the obvious danger of distraction:

"Course members were very ready to accept the working model as relevant to the role of the leader. Some difficulty, however, was experienced in getting members to act as observers. This was because there was a danger of the task involved becoming the main topic of interest. The instructor then had to bring observers back to the role of observing *leadership* rather than trying to solve the problem. This was particularly true of the Mast Exercise. This continued despite a very careful briefing on the purpose of the exercises.**"**

On the other hand, Caterpillar Tractor and others have found that thorough briefing and experienced trainers can mitigate this hazard:

"Our experience of handling the ACL course with management people had stressed the real importance of good briefing before attendance at the weekend conferences. It must be emphasized to them that the exercises and case studies in which they participate are a means to an end, not an end in themselves. By all means enjoy the experience, but relate it carefully to the objective of the conference—which is to identify leadership in action. In addition, we learned not to mix levels of management in this type of training'. If criticism is to be offered frankly this can result in rather raw experiences for the criticized. This is best handled by groups of equal status.**

Nor was information about the exercises handed on by participants to future course members, as some feared might happen. The Glasgow plant of Caterpillar confirm this :

Initially we were worried that the 'secrets' of the exercise would be 'leaked' in conversation by those who had already participated to those still to go. Surprisingly, we have no evidence that this is happening and it is obvious that all those who have already attended are reacting to the tutor's request to 'be like Dad—keep Mum'.

There is no reason why organizations should not develop their own exercises. This inventiveness has been positively encouraged, and many organizations have either substantially altered the exercises or have invented new ones. For example, Reed International Ltd have rewritten the £20 000 Fund exercise into one involving the purchase of vending machines, and have introduced into it some budgetary considerations. Again, Cadbury Ltd, has introduced into ACL training the Model Town Exercise, an interesting town planning project which verges, however, in the context of ACL training on being a case study.

Clearly it is easier to *adapt* or change written exercises; it is much harder to think up new practical exercises—ones which involve some element of *doing* as opposed to talking. The tasks in these exercises should not be trivial. As the 'action' has to be visible to the observers, the objects used have to be above a certain size. It must not be too easy (a common criticism of the Magazine Sorting Exercise), nor should it take up too much time. A good example of such a new exercise is the Trolley Assembling Problem developed by Ray Shaw at Fisons Ltd.

Originally, Functional Leadership included outdoor exercises. These were justified because of the nature of a military officer's work, and because going out of doors was a potent symbol to the officer cadet of the relevance of leadership training to the demands of his job in the field. Early ACL courses included one exercise of this kind involving planks and drums, and I am still a believer in them—especially with young course members.

Some trainers believe that open countryside is required for such exercises, but the Staff Training Department in the John Lewis Partnership is among those who have retained it, despite the location of the firm in London's busy Oxford Street.

" The Planks and Drums exercise is used on fine days! We perform this on the roof of our building. It is particularly good for highlighting the contrasting attitudes of men and women at work. The nature of the equipment tends to bring this out—males doing the lifting and carrying and females experiencing frustration by what they perceive as suppression from the male workers. This is most evident in the feedback discussion phase and it can easily be related to on-the-job situations."

Brathay Hall, the outdoor centre in the Lake District, as well as Endeavour Training, have pioneered courses based on the ACL concept but also involving adventure training, the creative arts, and social service for young managers and apprentices. The possibilities of such training for more senior executives, incorporating more practical and outdoor activity than the ACL Tutor's Manual originally envisaged, have already been explored by one enthusiastic managing director. In conjuction with sessions on decision-making, communicating, and creative thinking, such training may have a wider future, although it may strike some chairbound readers (from this report by Duff Hart-Davis in *The Sunday Telegraph* of 14 May 1972) as a form of shock therapy treatment!

Considering that their day began at 7 a.m. with a run, a game of volley-ball, and a round of the ropes-course, they are not looking too bad. But now these five businessmen and one police superintendent are in a bit of a predicament, marooned on an island in Windermere. 'You've been washed up on a barren shoreline,' says their instructor cheerfully, 'there's the mainland, over there'—he points to a rocky headland 60 yards away—'and there's your tackle. None of you can swim, and anyway the water's full of sharks. In 90 minutes there's going to be a tidal wave. So you'd better look lively.'

They set to. The tackle includes ropes, a pulley, a few sticks, two huge polythene bags, a bow and some arrows, and a light line. Obvious beginning : to shoot a line-carrying arrow on to the mainland. . . .

Elsewhere in the grounds of Brathay Hall, another group is struggling

104

to heave its own members over a seven-foot 'electrified barbed-wire fence' with strange affinities to the Berlin Wall. *Their* tackle—a few short poles, some string and a second, much bigger barrel—seems hopelessly inadequate; but according to David Gilbert-Smith, the wily ex-Special Air Service officer who devised the tests, the task is perfectly possible. A third group is in even worse difficulties trying to bridge a river. Adventure training for executives? The course is the invention of Mr Peter Prior, Group Managing Director of H. P. Bulmer, the Herefordshire cider-making firm.

Two trial runs at Brathay Hall last year were so successful that they are being repeated and extended this summer, with the help and advice of The Industrial Society. Most of the 'students' are executives from Bulmer's, aged between 25 and 50, but a leavening of outsiders is brought in. The central aim is to teach Action-Centred Leadership, but the courses include a considerable amount of tough outdoor activity, such as mountaineering, rock-climbing and underwater swimming.

'What I'm trying to do, is give people opportunities for achievemen', says Mr Prior. 'You may say—and plenty of people *do* say—"What the hell has underwater swimming got to do with industry?" Well, I believe that learning some entirely new skill gives an individual new confidence, and that when he gets back, it brushes off on his work. I believe our experiment has opened up entirely new ground in management training.'

Already some other large companies have shown keen interest in a project of this kind. Whether they join in or not, it may be that Bulmer's experiment will prove a shot-in-the-arm for adventure training as a whole.

Since 1972, the staffs of Brathay Hall and Bulmer's personnel department have further developed the contents of the course. More emphasis now falls on ACL training; less on the purely physical endurance element. At least three other major companies—all ACL users—have also joined in the experiment, sending teams of five or six managers on the courses in 1973.

In summary, it is important in the early stages of ACL to maintain the distinction between the leadership and the technical aspects of the practical observation exercises. There should be a progression from the non-technological to the kinds of projects or small tasks which might be encountered in a particular organization, always provided that they include the dimension of working with or directing a group of individuals in a team effort. The mixtures of practical exercises and written case studies of varying lengths, and of non-technical to technical tasks, should be judiciously made, according to the mental understanding and creative imagination of the course members. It is not always to be assumed that supervisors and foremen are devoid of these gifts : we tend to underestimate considerably the unused potential of managers at all ages and levels.

CAN POST-COURSE APPLICATION BE IMPROVED?

Both Functional Leadership and ACL courses end with an application session in which members have the opportunity to discuss and formulate an individual programme for using ACL in the immediate future. This session is designed to consolidate learning, expose further training needs in this sphere, and harvest the practical intentions with which the participants may have equipped themselves. An experienced and skilled tutor can comment on these projected actions, testing the substance of them and perhaps provoking new possibilities by mentioning examples of action that have followed previous courses. It is a vital part of this session for each participant to hear the proposed applications of others.

In the Sandhurst context it was easy for the instructor to follow up these proposed applications with some sort of informal appraisal session. Conditions in industry make it more difficult to provide this monitoring of the essential process of application, and some organizations have actively explored ways of ensuring or strengthening the 'down-to-earth' relevance of ACL when the person concerned gets back to the job.

One such experiment in involving line managers in the process and follow-up to ACL training is reported by the John Lewis Partnership.

"In the continuing development of training/line management relationships, we were having dialogues with managers which raised points like :

● Can you find a course for my manager?
● My manager needs help in. . . .
● During talks with my manager, it became evident that he wanted to. . . .

From this we assumed we were being asked for help and that department managers had a real desire to help develop their own subordinates. To managers with whom we had this sort of dialogue, and who had

106

attended an ACL course, we suggested running a three-day ACL course for *their* subordinates. However, we wanted the manager to play an active role, indeed become involved with the success of the course, by taking part as an observer/tutor with a trainer acting as controller.

All the managers agreed, albeit with apprehension. Before the event each of them briefed his subordinate, agreeing on which management skill he would concentrate on developing. These areas were made known to Training Department, so that we could make specific comment and offer feedback to help fulfill each individual's needs. Areas of skills nominated were, for example :

- planning
- delegation
- communication
- deployment of staff

Prior to the course, managers were asked to attend an observation session. (This in itself was helping us meet one of management's stated needs.) At this session we gave managers practice at observing a group on an ACL task. This was achieved through the use of a video-recording; we had previously recorded a task being done by a group of visitors (having asked their permission to do so). No manager observed his own subordinate as a leader.

On the last afternoon we provided time for each manager and his subordinate to meet in private and set one to three targets and a project which were mutually agreeable. The targets would be assessed at the end of three months, where the first-line managers would meet again to validate their development. The project in our view, required that notes or a diary should be kept.

After two weeks a meeting was held with managers who had participated and the question asked was : How do you think you did? Their answers could be summarized as :

- we are just beginners at the art of observing
- we realize the skill needed to be able to phrase comments which encourage rather than discourage

All believed that, with practice, they would improve and benefit, and they wanted opportunity to do so. They all were most aware of the difficulty in leaving their 'management hats' behind and how this inhibited the creation of a supportive climate. They agreed that this had great relevance to the everyday situation and could usefully be worked on, by themselves in their departments.

The immediate feedback is most encouraging and the experiment was well worth while. It gave us a feedback of how acceptable the concepts of line management involvement and responsibility for development are becoming."

At the foreman and supervisor level it is possible to get a great deal more out of the final session of ACL by going into the practical outcomes of the training in detail with individuals. The Industrial Society reported one interesting experiment at Mather and Platt Ltd, a Manchester-based engineering group :

66 During the follow-up day in their series of ACL courses, the foremen and office supervisors produced their own version of a leadership checklist. Ultimately, they ended up with a printed 'Code of Practice' which was compiled by the Foremen's Leadership Courses held at the University of Keele in 1971. This booklet is now in common use as part of the induction training of new foremen."

By contrast Reed International drew on the TWI (Training Within Industry) courses for some definite actions :

66 Another of our significant developments has been at the supervisor end of the spectrum. Here, a problem was felt in that—although the injunction to meet individual and team needs was sound—what seemed to be missing was some clear, crisp 'hows'. To meet this need, a marriage has evolved between basic ACL and the traditional TWI Job Relations approach. Thus, the TWI 'Supervisor Gets Results Through People' proposals are developed as some practical 'hows' to meet individual needs. The TWI 'Four Step' pattern for approaching human problems provides a further 'how'."

Another possibility at all levels of management is the employment of *project* work after the course as an aid to 'earthing' the training. At supervisory level the project can be structured and limited in time. For example, the Post Office have embraced such a method :

66 The course is rounded off with a project lasting some two days. This project is wide ranging and is based on the interrelation between mythical company (based on fact) and the Postal Business. Built-in rules and constraints together with choice factors force the students to exercise and practice all the concepts covered during the training

programme. It also helps the students to see that such skills and techniques are practical and are relevant to their work situation."

At all levels of management, post-course project work will be enhanced if the ACL course is expanded to include decision-making, problem-solving, and creative thinking. One company that has pioneered such an expansion (but still keeping the course under five days in length) is Whitbreads. The part played by project work after the course is described by Reginald Fitzgerald and Peter Bracher:

" To relate the course to their working lives, members were each asked to identify a real problem which existed in their own department and these were discussed in terms of the ACL concept of *task*, *group needs*, and *individual needs*. They were also asked to undertake a project to be completed when they returned to their place of work.

The project work proved to be most successful both as a learning experience for the course members and as a means of making tangible savings for the company. Each student selected his own project and discussed it with the company training officer during the week. He was encouraged to define his objectives in quantifiable terms and in many cases this led to difficulties, as it became apparent that much work still had to be done to assess the projects in measurable terms.

Company training officers gave a lot of help with the completion of the projects and senior management showed an encouraging degree of co-operation. Progress on the projects was reported and assessed at a follow-up meeting six months later. These meetings were taken by Whitbread's group training staff and were also attended by top management from the companies concerned within the group. Top management had an opportunity at these meetings to appreciate the content and style of the course. The assessment of the projects showed that, even on the most conservative estimate, total savings had been made that showed a return on the cost of the training of around 400 per cent.

The lessons learnt in the assessment of the course have provided a signpost for future development; the experience gained from the project work has shown that this is a training method which could be more extensively used in the future. It would be interesting to experiment with projects tackled by a team rather than an individual. It is possible to envisage project work supplemented by a series of counselling tutorials during which the concepts normally taught in the classroom would be discussed, replacing the conventional type of training."

The project method makes considerable demands in time on training staff and line management, but it can be both practically useful and educationally valuable—providing the quality of tutoring is high. The danger is that project work will become so widespread (already more than half of Britain's management teachers use it) that it will set up its own tidal reaction. Employed indiscriminately, without proper preparation, support and evaluation, the project approach can do no good at all.

One merit in *well-conducted* project work is that it offers a financially quantifiable method of evaluating training, which is all to the good. But projects, which in effect extend the period of study, can never replace the more direct application of ACL to a person's customary or habitual attitudes and actions. Moreover, the improvements in overall leadership in an organization, *the intended outcome of ACL*, are not easy to capture in even an interrelated series of quantifiable projects. These cautionary words, however, do not diminish my own enthusiasm for this enjoyable and effective method of education as a supplementary 'bridge' between training and the working environment.

There is sufficient evidence that, where ACL is applied, it does influence the orientation, attitudes, and actions of those who take part in it. The extent to which this happens will always depend on such variables as the organization, the quality of the course members, and the competence and leadership of the tutorial staff. Such factors existing, no course designed can guarantee the proper 'earthing' of the contents. It is natural for trainers to question whether everything possible has been done to help a course member to see the relevance of what he has learnt and practised, short of interfering with the sacred right of rejection. At lower levels of management this may entail compiling lists of examples of experience drawn from previous courses; in the higher reaches, project work has a part to play in buttressing the bridge spanning the worlds of principle and practice. At all levels, throughout the training a wise tutor will point frequently to the obvious need for tangible results in the course member's own organization and its environment which should follow the course.

CONCLUSIONS

In this chapter we have considered some of the questions which arise when those using ACL (or about to use it) set about their own method of getting the best out of it. In a sense the debates and issues discussed briefly above are tactical matters. There remain two strategic conclusions.

110

First, the better the ACL tutor the more that will come out of the training. 'Pilot error' sometimes explains why courses do not perform as well as they should, although it is tempting and human to blame it on the content or methods. Although ACL is designed to be resistant to pilot error, so that it rarely crashes, it saves its best results for those who (as Oliver Cromwell put it) 'know what they are fighting for, and love what they know'. In the past five years I have been fortunate enough to see ACL courses led by masters of its intentions and techniques, and it was impossible to doubt that good results would ensue.

Second, ACL produces its best results when it is fully integrated into an organization. Ideally this means that directors should be among the first course members, or at least that senior management should be involved from the start. All levels and functions should eventually take part. Links should be forged with other current approaches, such as Management by Objectives or target-centred training tailored to the needs of the company, weaving ACL into a total philosophy. The course member is then in no danger of forgetting the concepts and skills he has begun to acquire, because he encounters them frequently in his daily working life.

Indeed Fred Patten, the present Head of The Industrial Society's Leadership Department, has reported a growing use of ACL as a change-agent for the whole organization. The simplicity of ACL allows it to be the basis for training and management education from shop floor to the boardroom, with the result that a common language relatively free from jargon gradually develops which reflects a shared vision of the enterprise. Arthur Guinness (Ireland), Rolls-Royce (1971), and Rio Tinto-Zinc are among the companies that report the benefits of such a multi-level strategy being adopted from the start. In Rolls-Royce (1971), for example, over 800 managers have already taken part in the ACL courses. Having done it himself from boardroom to shop floor levels Fred Patten reports:

> **❝** I have never found any difficulty over the acceptance of ACL even with most experienced and senior of executives because they could see with clarity the common sense practicality of the approach. The same practical relevance appeals at all other levels including that of the shop floor foreman. **❞**

It is always difficult to evaluate the wider effects of training on a company's performance, but the results at Ilford Ltd, for example, persuaded a sister company—Clayton Aniline Ltd—to ask the Leadership Department for ten courses in five weeks, specifically in order to bring about a change in the ethos of their management at all levels.

111

In conclusion, it is always possible to improve ACL, to get better results from it. Not only is it still a very young form of training, but it is also deliberately left incomplete or unfinished, so that organizations may have the fun of adapting it to their specific situation. These creative changes, coupled with the ever-growing professionalism of management educators and trainers, will ensure that organizations get the best results they possibly can from the ACL approach in the future.

6. Developing ACL

Developing ACL

In its earlier forms the ACL course lasted between one and two days. The explicit teaching or content in the Task and Team Maintenance (or Group Needs) circles, centred upon the concept of *functions*, such as briefing, planning, controlling, evaluating, setting, and maintaining group standards (or norms) and encouraging the group. In the Individual Needs circle the theories of Maslow and Herzberg formed the main reference

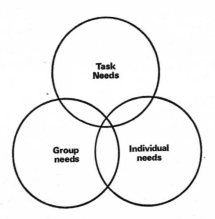

points. It could be said that this simple approach, if properly put over and then supported by practical observation and discussion, would give course members at least the bare bones of leadership in management. At the cost of lengthening the course, however, it would be possible to go into any or all of the three circles in greater depth. Whether or not it is profitable to do so depends on the consideration of six general factors which seem to be involved in all human communication, of which a management course is only one example.[1] Before considering in more detail the extension of ACL we should briefly review these factors.

115

Aim. It is not always easy to state clearly the intention behind a course. If one defines it too closely or specifically, as some have advocated, there is a danger that the outcome becomes too predetermined. The results may be measurable, but they may also be extremely limited in consequence. On the other hand too wide a scope in the wording of the intention encourages a genial vagueness in all concerned. The solution lies in a combination of *Aim* and *Objectives*, the former being more general and the latter more specific. The concept of an *Aim*, as opposed to an *Objective*, allows the trainer to be pleasantly surprised by some practical or definite outcomes which were not planned for or envisaged by his *Objectives* (goals or targets) for the course, but which do fall well within the broader scope of the Aim.[2]

Before considering a substantial development of the ACL course it is important to be clear on what are the Aim and Objectives of training in this leadership or human relations field. Does the trainer need to give the manager or supervisor a store of conceptual knowledge of sociology, social psychology, and so on; if so, how much? How important is the other kind of knowledge, which for want of a better term we could call experimental knowledge? What degree of 'sensitivity to group processes', for example, does a course member need to do his job effectively? How much of this experiential knowledge can or should be acquired in the relatively artificial and costly setting of a training course? These questions require carefully judged answers before more detailed planning begins.

The Course Members. These questions have also naturally led us to consider the capabilities and expectations of the students or participants. It is just as easy to overestimate in others their interests, ability, and appetite for all but the essential or necessary knowledge of human relations as it is to underestimate them. Perhaps the answer lies in always looking closely at the job, actual or in the near future, for which the student is preparing himself. If the course designer cannot articulate the relevance of that proposed extension of ACL—be it a research finding or a theory—to the present or imminent roles of those on the course, then it should be left on the optional reading list or handout.

Owing to the recent mushroom growth of the behavioural sciences, some managers in organizations have become rather like those Athenians whom St Paul encountered of whom it was recorded that they 'had no time for anything but talking or hearing about the latest novelty'. It is important to distinguish between the artificial wants of these so-called

116

'sophisticated' managers and the natural needs of their jobs. In other words, because course members want or expect a spate of novel theories and research conclusions, this in itself is not a sufficient argument for providing them. It may be that such managers need more time and practice in applying what they know already in exercises, case-studies, or projects. Sometimes this Athenian appetite for new ideas as ends in themselves is the result of a large organization having uncritically gorged itself on the behavioural sciences in the early or middle years of the 1960s. In such cases the remedy is not to include more content but to concentrate on application and evaluation.

The Content. Setting aside the merely novel, the latest fashion, there still remains a considerable body of interesting material which might augment the basic instruction in each of the three circles. Although such material may not merit the title of tried-and-proven knowledge it has survived the test of two or three decades, keeping its head above the torrent of publications, packages and patter which have been handed down the mountain since the 1930s.

The issue at this point is whether or not ACL should retain its primary concern with *training* as opposed to *education*.

According to one dictionary, *education* has the general meaning of 'strengthening of the powers of body or mind', while *training* is 'to prepare for performance, by instruction, practice or otherwise'. Obviously education is more general and we should expect to find in it more background and less essential knowledge, so that a student knows more about the evidences upon which practical principles rest and the processes by which they were discovered.

It is beyond the scope of this book to enter into the management education *versus* management training debate, except to offer the conclusion that there is a place for both. Nor need it be assumed that they should be pursued separately. It is as possible to include elements of management education in in-company training, as it is to introduce training courses into the longer time-span educational programmes.[3]

Two points can be made about ACL in industry. First, there are bodies of management knowledge or practice, such as Management by Objectives, which are both relevant to the training situation and naturally complementary to the basic ACL content and approach. Secondly, there is no reason why the distinction between 'education' and 'training' should not be blurred in practice as long as the course tutors and members appreciate the distinction; indeed there are some training situations which invite the infusion of a wider educational approach. In such cases the trefoil model takes on the additional role of an integrating model, an aspect of its usefulness which will be fully discussed later.

The Situation. A particular organization may suggest—or even dictate—that one or other of the three circles should receive extra emphasis, both in conceptual treatment and in practical application. It may be, for example, that one firm has been excessively task-centred, and its leaders may need to concentrate, temporarily, more upon the creation of a genuine *esprit de corps*, based on the exercise of team maintenance functions. Or technological change, and the consequent restructuring of the groups in the organization or industry, may have created acute problems for individuals, so that the leader needs a much fuller understanding of the individual than a summary of Maslow and Herzberg can provide.

The Methods. As we have seen, there is no particular merit in introducing new methods to teach the basics of an ACL course. The exercises, films and case studies may become very familiar to the teacher but they come fresh to the students on each new course. It is important that any new content or supplementary material should share the same participatory training methods as the rest of the ACL course. An inserted chunk of monologue lecturing, for example, will not be well received in a course which elsewhere eschews such methods. One must look for congruity of method as well as content.

The Course Tutor. Going back to origins again, it is worth recalling that ACL was designed to be taught by 'line managers', the Sandhurst company commander on a two- or three-year tour of duty from his regiment or corps. Similarly, Industrial Society advisers, for the most part, are line or personnel managers who will return to general duties after about three years of training and advisory work. In many organizations the training role is still a secondment from line management; in many others the management of education and training has become a professional commitment with its own career structure. Sometimes, a secondment is long enough for a training manager to specialize, to acquire a professionalism in the best sense of that word. Clearly, the extra knowledge and competence of a trainer, suitably attested by others, is a new (but not the only) factor in any decision on the further development of the ACL course in a particular setting.

118

A consideration of all the above six factors taken together should lead to a sound judgement on the extension or development of ACL training in any given context. Such is the flexibility of the approach that it can be expanded or contracted according to the needs of the situation. Indeed such adaptations are a means by which the course tutors can teach leadership and decision-making by example as well as by precept. What now remains is to consider some of the more obvious ways in which ACL can be developed in each of its three main over-lapping areas of concern : Task, Group, and Individual.

MANAGEMENT BY OBJECTIVES

Management by Objectives (or MBO) has achieved a world-wide reputation in all kinds of organizations : retailing, manufacturing, and service industries; small family concerns, giant corporations, and local and central government. In its simplest form it consists of a manager sitting down and agreeing goals or targets with a subordinate or a team for a limited period of time, say, six months. The old-fashioned approach consisted of the manager simply telling his subordinate what to do, possibly on a day-to-day basis.

As the leading exponent of the more developed form of MBO, John Humble grounded it squarely on the philosophy of Douglas McGregor and Frederick Herzberg, seeing it as

> 'a dynamic system which seeks to integrate the company's need to clarify and achieve its profit and growth goals with the manager's need to contribute and develop himself. It is a demanding and rewarding style of managing a business.'[4]

Adopting the systems approach which became much more current in the 1960s, John Humble saw MBO as 'a worthwhile system' in an organization where there is 'a continuous process' involving seven interdependent and dynamic techniques :

- Reviewing critically and restating the Company's *Strategic and Tactical Plans.*
- Clarifying with each manager the *Key Results and Performance Standards* he must achieve, in line with unit and company objectives, and gaining his contribution and commitment to these.
- Agreeing with each manager a *Job Improvement Plan* which makes a measurable and realistic contribution to the unit and company plans for better performance.

119

- Providing conditions in which it is possible to achieve the Key Results and Improvement Plans, notably :
  an *organization structure* which gives a manager maximum freedom and flexibility in operation;
  management control information in a form and at a frequency which makes for more effective self-control and better and quicker decisions.
- Using systematic *Performance Review* to measure and discuss progress towards results and *Potential Review* to identy men with potential for advancement.
- Developing *Management Training Plans* to help each manager to overcome his weaknesses, to build on his strengths and to accept a responsibility for self-development.
- Strengthening a manager's motivation by effective *selection, salary,* and *succession plans.*

Management by Objectives can be made into a yet more fully-fledged or 'sophisticated' system by the use of complicated forms and charts, and built-in checks and safeguards. The problem with such advanced systems is that they require equally elaborate management training in order to make them work. The 'human factor' in the shape of inadequately trained managers or new staff often leads to break-downs in such systems. Better to keep MBO as simple as possible while still retaining the disciplines which are implied in the very notion of a system, and which are clearly justified by the nature of the common task and the corporate and individual needs of the organization's members.

Coming to the relation of ACL to MBO, there is evidence that some companies have used ACL as a preliminary to installing MBO as a system. There is justification in some organizations for employing this strategy. John Humble has pointed out more than once that *leadership* is not only a necessary prerequisite for making MBO worthwhile—it is also sometimes essential for its very introduction :

> 'It takes time, patience, and leadership and conviction from the top, to evolve a new set of attitudes. Unfortunately, many companies are in a hurry to get the mechanics of the system introduced and are reluctant to make the investment of time and resources to do a thorough job in changing attitudes.'[5]

With good reason John Humble laid a special stress on the leadership of the chief executive as the key to such a necessary change in the climate or ethos of an organization :

'No one suggests that personal leadership is the *only* requirement, nor that the chief executive is an entirely free agent to do what he wishes. In fact, his leadership is really educational in generating purposefulness, creativity, and a commitment to company goals among his team. So often in practice we see that this man's courage and example can set the whole tone of the business. . . .'

Despite his own 'unique contribution'—or perhaps through it—the chief executive can do much to create the leadership required if MBO is to be a matter of the spirit as well as the letter, by introducing ACL training first. For ACL can bring about the changes in understanding and attitudes at all levels of management which can make MBO appear not as an abrogation of 'tough' management authority but as its fulfilment in a challenging, demanding, and disciplined form of leadership applicable in virtually every kind of enterprise.

On the other hand, many companies and organizations have adopted ACL *after* introducing a version of MBO into their daily management practice. In terms of the basic ACL course we can identify three major reasons why this might be deemed a good idea :

- First, from John Humble's remarks quoted above, it is clear that the MBO approach implies a high standard of leadership at *all* levels of management. And ACL offers a simple and direct way of stimulating thought about appropriate leadership, initiating new action, and furthering the development of leadership potential in the long term.
- Second, ACL directs attention to the importance of setting objectives in the Group (or Team Maintenance) and Individual Needs circles as well as the Task one. Without the interlocking three circles model MBO can easily relapse into being an exclusively 'task-centred' technique.
- Third, elements in ACL help to explain *why* MBO is important. For example, the Tannenbaum and Schmidt chart (Fig. 1.2, page 14) underlines the common-sense fact that the more people share in decisions which affect their working lives the more they will tend to feel responsible for implementing them. (This is also true about the concept of Purpose, Aims and Objectives, rapidly becoming part of the ACL content, which helps people to see objectives in their wider context.)

121

Kalamazoo Limited is a medium-sized company employing nearly 2000 people. It designs, produces, and sells business systems for industry and commerce. Based at Birmingham (where it employs some 1600 people) it also has some 45 sales branches throughout the UK. From these branches nearly 300 salesmen sell Kalamazoo systems. By the late 1960s the company had already adopted Target Setting, a form of MBO. Michael Amies describes the impact of ACL on this established practice :

" As part of an effort to develop future managers, we ran a regular series of three-day seminars for groups of potential managers. These seminars consisted of lectures, exercises, discussions, and a one-day management game. In January 1969 the principle of ACL was first introduced. The effect of this approach upon the pace and depth of our three-day course was immediate, and the relationship of some of the ACL concepts to the work being done on target setting within the Company also became very clear from the outset.

The targets that had been set within the Company since the introduction of the target setting scheme had been largely in the task area. In other words our managers had paid little attention to the two other important areas of their job : the *team* that they were leading and the *individuals* who made up that team. Similarly, many of the Job Descriptions that we had been writing, virtually ignored these two aspects of a manager's responsibility.

These two facts suggested that ACL training should be more widely applied in the Company. First, it reinforced strongly the approach to setting targets which we were trying to persuade our managers to adopt. Second, it was a type of training to which participants responded enthusiastically, and which they seemed to be able to relate very readily to their own job situation.

So that we could learn more about ACL, the Personnel Director and myself (the Training Manager) attended a one-day appreciation course at which John Adair described the aims and methods of this type of training, and conducted one of the observation exercises. Subsequently, Dr Adair conducted a one-day appreciation course within the Company, to judge whether ACL could be expanded for all managers. This course was attended by 15 of the Company's top managers, including the Managing Director. Following this we ran two-day courses for all managers, in groups of peers, starting at the top and finishing with first-line supervision.

122

We had four main objectives :

- To make managers more effective in their jobs, and thus improve the Company's performance.
- To improve the quality and range of the targets set for managers.
- To create a better understanding between the various divisions of the Company by bringing members of each together on the same course.
- To involve senior line managers in the running of the courses so that they could better get to know (and be known by) the members of their divisions.

We never considered this training as a one-off exercise. It was seen essentially as part of the existing system of target setting and we related it directly to our form of MBO in the final summary session. We also revised Job Descriptions to ensure that the manager's attention was focused on the group and individual needs as well as the task needs.

So that the manager would be reminded frequently of the lessons of the course, a card follow-up system was developed. A master card again posed the question 'What are you going to do?', and then gave some reminder questions under each of the three ACL headings (Task, Group and Individual).

Each manager received his first card in the week following attendance on the course. Thereafter once a month for 12 months he received a further reminder card which asked him a specific question under one of the headings concerning his follow-up application of the course.

By this means, among other more conventional methods such as personal contact, we set out to maintain the manager's application of ACL within the framework of the target setting system.**"**

DECISION-MAKING, PROBLEM-SOLVING AND CREATIVE THINKING

Another way of developing ACL training is to incorporate within its scope some sessions on making the most effective use of the mental resources available to the leader. Every individual has 10 000 million or more brain cells, so that the potential thinking power present in even a small team or group is enormous. An introductory session (or ninety-minute period) can be fruitfully spent on presenting the 'raw materials' or basic processes of human thought : analysing, synthesizing, and valuing; the part played by the depth (or less conscious) mind; and the positive and negative influences of emotion. With suitable short practical exercises,

123

such a session can alert the attention of the participants to the vital 'thinking' aspect of a manager's job.

All these fundamental movements of the mind have to come into play when a decision is being made. Decisions directly concern the Task circle, for the manager has to clarify constantly his Purpose, Aims and Objectives, review the relevant factors, define and evaluate the courses or policies open to him, and choose one of them. Then he has to implement the decision and cope with both the anticipated and also the unexpected consequences. Moreover, the manager should understand the range of possibilities for sharing decisions and the factors to be weighed (consciously or in the depth mind) in deciding how to decide with the maximum involvement of others. Lastly, his decision-making or judgement about people can be explored and perhaps improved to the benefit of all concerned in any organization.

Thus the kind of training in decision-making which belongs or fits naturally with ACL is a long way removed from the contents of most books which have 'decision' in their titles but turn out to be volumes on statistics, economic theory, or the laws of chance. This is also true of the proposed approach to *problem solving*. The concern of the leader and his team is how to tackle the problems which crop up like obstacles in the path which they hope is taking them towards the attainment of their immediate objective. Thus engineering problems, or systems that have temporarily broken down, occupy only a small percentage of the leader's or group's time. Yet most of the literature on the subject concentrates on this type of problem. Therefore, it is too limited to merit the attention of the practical leader or manager. But it is possible to introduce him to some general rules and one or two general problem-solving strategies, as well as providing such practical exercises as to ensure these sessions should not fall out of character with the basic ACL course in both content and method.

As John Humble has pointed out, the ability to be *creative* belongs essentially to the art of leadership, especially in conditions of rapid technological and social change. This aspect includes the educational talent for 'drawing out' the creative thinking latent in a group or (in the case of the chief executive) in the whole organization. Creative thinking can throw up new aims and objectives, new plans and methods, or new products in the Task area. In the Team Maintenance circle the creative or contructive person can do much to build up human relations in unexpected and fresh ways. With regard to Individual Needs a creative mind can often sense the unused potential in individuals, and challenge

124

the best from them by such creative methods as restructuring jobs into more interesting and demanding responsibilities.

It would be a mistake to equate creative thinking with 'brainstorming'. This latter technique, however, although it plays a relatively small part in actual creative thinking, is a very good teaching method. As such it forms a useful introduction to the leadership of creative thinking of problem-solving groups. And such is the flexibility required by enterprises if they are to survive and progress, that any team or work group should be able to be turned into a creative thinking or problem-solving group.

In 1970, Whitbread Ltd invited me to evolve, with their training staff, a short course on decision-making, problem-solving, and creative thinking as a development of the basic ACL model. This course, which lasted five days, included educational sessions on the behavioural sciences, in an introductory day, which was then followed by two days of ACL and one and a half days of Effective Thinking (as it could be called). Initially evolved as a series of middle-management courses, they were later condensed into a form suitable for Whitbread's Group Board, and the managing directors of operating companies within the group.

Several other companies using ACL have already adopted, adapted, or experimented with, one or more of the Effective Thinking sessions. The most comprehensive application so far has been accomplished by the National Westminster Bank on junior management courses. With the skilled help of assistant tutors, and a carefully planned combination of small group and plenary sessions, they cater for numbers double or treble the normal ACL-course size of 15 to 25 members. Moreover, they have not only introduced new case studies, but have pioneered the use of the film *Twelve Angry Men* as an 'observation exercise' to highlight the major forms of applied thinking. After two experimental courses (I attended the second of these) the ratings on the third and subsequent courses have steadily improved. 'The gap has now narrowed on Action-Centred Leadership,' writes David Despres (who manages the junior courses) 'which has always been considered by course members, in their review of the course, as the most beneficial of all the sessions.'

Communication
In *Training for Communication* I suggested some ways in which ACL can be developed by incorporating in it—or relating to it—a short practical course on communication. Whitbread Ltd invited me to test these sessions by designing, with the central training staff, a five-day course

on communication (as a follow-up for those who had taken part in ACL training) and by leading the first two days and the last half day.

It is vital that the ACL hall-marks of simplicity, clarity, variety, direct relevance, and participation should be maintained in the communication field of extension. Without going into detail on the actual contents and methods of each session it is sufficient here to summarize the main topics that might merit serious attention for possible inclusion :

- The Nature of Communication (Non-Verbal, Role of Language; Six factors in the 'Communication Star')
- The Four Basic Skills
    Speaking (The Search for Rules; Five Principles; Audio-Visual Aids)
    Listening (Symptoms of Poor listening; Steps to Better Listening)
    Writing (Style; Better Usage; Word Power; Letters; Reports)
    Reading (Reading Speeds; Guidelines for Reading; A Strategy for Study)
- Communication in Organizations (Effects of Size and Change; Some Models; Priorities; Some Key Methods; Corporate Integrity)
- Leadership of Meetings (Communication in Small Groups; Kinds of Meeting; Leadership Functions; Conference Leadership; Leadership Manner)
- Appraisal Interviews (Difficult Conversations; Praise and Criticism; Presenting the Case; Receiving End)

This list is not exhaustive, but it does suggest some of the main topics which can increase a leader's general awareness, understanding, and skill by focusing training attention on the key communication aspects of his responsibility.

These possibilities have been demonstrated on The Industrial Society's five-day course *The Manager as a Leader*. Devised by Elizabeth Andrews and developed by Nigel Nicholls, this course is intended for senior managers and executives, and for younger managers of high potential. Nigel Nicholls has described its scope :

“ In general terms its purpose is to develop the manager's ability to get the best from the people who work for him. Because it is residential and the sessions go on until late in the evening, there is a greater opportunity to achieve this purpose more fully and comprehensively than its nominal length of $5\frac{1}{2}$ days might suggest.

126

Action-Centred Leadership plays a prominent part in the course—indeed the course is built round it. First, it is used as an introduction—to open the mind of each course member so that he looks again at what he exists to achieve and how he does it. It establishes a state of mind that is more receptive, without being uncritically accepting, of all that follows in the course.

The second purpose of using ACL is to provide the overall framework of management into which the remainder of the course fits. Thus rather than appearing as separate, disconnected subjects, each in its own watertight compartment, ACL draws these threads together to form a natural, logical whole. To underline this point further, certain techniques of management introduced in one session reappear at intervals throughout the course.

As well as examining the work of the behavioural scientists to see to what extent their findings can be applied by individual course members, various techniques which are intended to help a manager become more effective are studied. The method employed here is short talks from lecturers who are experts in their fields, coupled with exercises in which everyone takes part.

First come sessions which look at the factors a manager must take into account in planning an organization structure. This leads naturally into role or job definitions and thus to the appraisal interview which itself leads to the closely similar skill of selection interviewing, and a practical exercise involving outside 'guinea pigs' is then staged. After this comes a look at the barriers to communication and the skills of presenting a case. Finally each course member works out how he is going to apply back in his job something of what he has studied and discussed on the course, and this he then presents to the course. The course finishes by refocusing on the three-circle diagram.**"**

Group Needs

Some organizations have already developed ACL by adding extra sessions (or expanding the present ones) which touch on the Group Needs or Team Maintenance circle. In the Whitbread's courses a social psychologist (Lady Margaret Brown) prefaced the ACL and Effective Thinking days with a general day on the behavioural sciences, especially the reasons for the formations of groups and their needs, illustrated by some 'leaderless' group exercises.[6] British Insulated Callender's Cables Ltd have also introduced ACL with a day on the social science background. Trevor Johnson writes :

" I feel that The Industrial Society course did not spend enough time on basic psychology, perhaps on the assumption that Maslow's and Herzberg's theories were already familiar material. This we did not find to be true. We therefore spend a whole day trying to relate the work of some behavioural scientists to John Adair's approach to leadership. Our experience is that the functional approach has a greater impact when introduced on the second day of the course. **"**

One way of developing ACL in this direction is by increasing the references to research and theoretical writings on the social psychology of work groups. A training manager in Hoover Ltd, for example, writes :

" Through time we have found that the major area which is not adequately covered by the ACL package is that of group needs. Consequently our main adaptation has been to include an introduction to the work of such people as Rensis Likert. This has simply meant adding one information session to the syllabus. **"**

One problem in this approach, if it was extended to further sessions, would be the relative ineffectiveness of hearing a lot of information *about* groups in contrast to the more direct knowledge gained by observation, experience, practice, and discovery in other parts of the course. But direct knowledge of group psychology (over and above the levels attainable in the structured group exercises, discussions, and film observation in the ACL course) suggests a move towards 'leaderless' or 'unstructured' discussion groups with the consequent higher degree of knowledge and competence requirement for the course tutor or trainer. The amount of time needed to make worthwhile progress also increases sharply, and with it the overall cost of the course.

Doubtless there are 'half-way houses' or various compromises between these two poles of 'information sessions' and forms of 'T-Groups' or group dynamics, with all the questionable assumptions that they tend to introduce into in-company training. One such solution is to improve the quality of observation and feedback in the ACL exercises by the use of such methods as sociometric diagrams (or 'communication flow charts'). Reed International Ltd have developed their version of ACL along these lines :

" A further strand in our 'Action-Centred Human Relations' course is the use of leaderless discussions early in the course to provide a potent basis for discussing group behaviour at the appropriate stage of the subject development.

128

Another concern we have had about the standard ACL approach is that its focus on the leader can over-emphasize the leader's role in the situation and thereby miss critical interactions between leader and team members. To fill this need, on courses where this level of sophistication can make a valid contribution, we introduce a Behavioural Analysis feedback using course tutors as observers, and construct 'Communication Flow Diagrams' to catch the pattern of relationships."[7]

It is interesting to reflect that in the early Functional Leadership courses at Sandhurst some company commanders spontaneously introduced leaderless groups early in the training. But again a note of caution needs to be sounded. To have the course tutors and their associates taking on the larger part of the observation would depart from one of the essentials of ACL, which is involving the course *members* fully through observing for themselves. These two sources of observation and comment (staff and members) are obviously not incompatible, but the balance always needs to be tilted heavily in favour of the participants.

Leaderless group exercises, developments in observation sheets (or check-lists), discussion, or films such as *Twelve Angry Men*: all these can play a part in improving the possibility of a deeper learning in the Group Needs or Team Maintenance circle. Closed circuit television and computer analysis of the spoken words may also have contributions to make. But in the training situation, as elsewhere, it is important to keep the sense of proportion suggested by the trefoil model of the three circles. It is easy for a trainer to get the bit between his teeth in one of the three areas and ignore or play down the other two. Special caution is needed in the area of Group Needs where we lack the theory or general principles which can be universally recommended as obviously relevant to the job of practical leadership. And experience in leaderless groups is useless if there are too few principles, common insights, or 'rules of thumb' which will facilitate transfer of learning to the workplace. If the only outcome is 'awareness' or 'sensitivity' we must first (to repeat the point) judge what levels or degrees of these states are essential to the practical manager as opposed, for example, to the social worker or to the teacher himself.

Individual Needs
As already noted, some organizations have augmented the ACL Individual Needs basic treatment with more attention to research into motivation, job satisfaction, and attitudes to work. Presenting the essential theories of both Maslow and Herzberg, as in ACL, is a foundation for

further developments in this area of management studies. Maslow and Herzberg can be explained simply with visual aids. To some extent they are alternatives, offering a choice of interpretation. Those with a mental dichotomizing tendency (tending to see things in sharp contrast) may prefer Herzberg's 'motivators' and 'hygiene factors'. Those with holistic minds, who see life in terms of unities or wholes, may choose the linear model of Maslow's 'hierarchy of needs', which presents no black-and-white divisions. To some extent, however, they complement each other in that Maslow prevents us from pressing Herzberg's useful distinction (useful at least for teaching purposes) into a false dichotomy, while Herzberg establishes the practical relevance of the more general view of human nature pioneered by Maslow and others to the actual world of the office, factory and shop-floor. Douglas McGregor's Theory X and Theory Y also serves to translate the underlying philosophy of 'self-actualization' into the organizational setting, but not in such specific terms as Herzberg and his colleagues.

One method of developing ACL would be to show some of the films and present more of the literature on individual needs and motivation. Above a certain level of training some of the suggested modifications of the early Herzberg findings could fruitfully be considered, especially those which highlight the positive contribution of leadership as a 'motivator' and not a negative 'hygiene factor'.[8] Or practical exercises in restructuring jobs could be tackled, and possibly related to sessions on creative thinking and to some study of the case histories of firms which have applied the 'job enrichment' approach.[9]

At this point training is beginning to merge into education. If this is judged appropriate it may well be worth considering the assumptions about 'self-actualization' which underlie this whole school. For example, by studying the ways in which sociological and cultural factors may shape an individual's or a group's perception of the nature of work in relation to human needs.[10] Such considerations may remind us that the concept of 'Individual Needs' (or Task or Group Needs for that matter) is not the total explanation behind human behaviour. That we shall never arrive at, but we can at least begin to indentify the key counterbalancing role played by *values* in work, especially the values intrinsic in the common purpose, social unity, and the individual person (as an end in himself or herself as well as being a means to corporate goals). It may be that in the last analysis, as Maslow thought, values are merely reflections of what the human organism, in its more mature forms, needs. On the other hand it may be that values are ultimately first, and it is because we value things,

130

people, or ourselves that they create a sense of need in us to respond appropriately to them.

These sentences illustrate some of the opportunities—and pitfalls—in going further into the theories and philosophies of motivation. Yet the models of Maslow and Herzberg, coupled with the decision-making continuum and an emphasis on the importance of a leadership which relates objectives and aims to a valuable (or worthwhile) purpose, give the practical manager enough understanding to reconsider the quality of his own leadership and possibly to identify some organizational or structural changes which could fruitfully be made in the interests of both the common task and the individuals concerned. Of that possibility there is plenty of evidence from those organizations which have adopted ACL training, if from no other source.

CONCLUSION

This chapter describes some of the actual or possible developments of ACL within the framework of the three circles. There are other possibilities. For example, more attention could be given to the influence of the *situation* on the relations of leader and team members. Again Reed International have begun to tackle this particular aspect :

66 We believe one weakness to be the thinness of the work on situational influences, and we have expanded this by discussion and illustrations. Accordingly, we stress that performance on the course is itself an illustration of *situational* leadership, and that therefore success or failure on the course is not a valid judgement of leadership in the back-home situation.99

The intention in this chapter has been to illustrate the possibilities rather than to define the limits of the ACL approach. ACL is a young form of training, with much life in it, and much of its appeal lies in the integrating role it can play at all levels of management training. It is this *integrating* potential, broadly within the context of training rather than education, that has formed the main argument in the chapter.

REFERENCES AND COMMENTS

1. See, John Adair, *Training for Communication*, chapter 1, MacDonald, (1973).
2. The distinction between purpose, aims and objectives is discussed in *Training for Decisions* (1971). The application of the Aims and Objectives in the training situation in particular is described by Ivor Davies, *The Management of Learning*, McGraw-Hill, (1971).

3. R. W. Revans, *Developing Effective Managers*, Praeger, (1971).
4. *Management by Objectives in Action*, ed. J. W. Humble, McGraw-Hill, (1970), 3.
5. *Ibid*, 18.
6. See, Margaret Brown, *The Manager's Guide to the Behavioural Sciences*, Industrial Society Notes for Managers, Number 16. Here Lady Brown relates the findings of contemporary behavioural science and organizational studies directly to the three-circles model.
7. Behaviour Analysis along these lines is described in N. Racham, *et al. Developing Interactive Skills*, Wellens, (1971).
8. For summaries of 'the Herzberg debate' and further discussion, see M. Argyle, *The Social Psychology of Work*, Penguin, (1972), and *Psychology at Work*, ed. P. B. Warr, Penguin, (1971), chapters 13 and 14.
9. For eight short case histories of 'job enrichment' (illustrating the variety of possible changes, the length of time involved, the critical importance of payment systems, and the possible pressures on management), see L. King-Taylor, *Not for Bread Alone: An Appreciation of Job Enrichment*, Business Books, (1972).
10. For an example of sociological influences see J. H. Goldthorpe, *et al. The Affluent Worker*, Cambridge University Press, (1968).

7. ACL and industrial relations

ACL and industrial relations

'What industry needs now is not bosses but leaders.'

Vic Feather, General Secretary, TUC

There is much wider recognition today that the prime responsibility for good industrial relations lies with management. In particular, the quality of managerial leadership is often mentioned as the most decisive single factor in creating and maintaining high productivity with human justice. It might be claimed that, by focusing attention upon leadership ability and demonstrating that there are practical ways of developing it, ACL is doing its share in bringing about long-term improvements in industrial relations.

The Trade Union Movement came into being first to protect the individual against exploitation in the name of the task, and later to promote or advance the individual's interest in a positive way. Thus, in terms of the three-circles model, the Trade Unions exist to hold a 'watching brief' over the Individual Needs circle in its relation with the other two (the needs of the task and the needs of the organization). Union leaders are elected and are accountable to their members for leading in this double work of protection and promotion.

The three-circle model, however, suggests that the Task, Group and Individual Needs circles overlap, but not entirely so. There is a *tension* between them, but not a *conflict*. It is important to explore the difference between these two states, starting from definitions, for it is more than an academic quibble over words : it is a matter of vital importance to us all.

The *Shorter Oxford English Dictionary* defines 'conflict' as 'an encounter with arms; a fight, especially a prolonged struggle'. In figurative use it suggests a collision or clash of incompatible interests. Under-

135

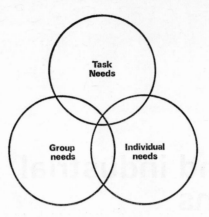

lying the word is the picture of two hostile forces or opposing interests, engaged in a battle or guerilla warfare until one has achieved victory over the other. In the minds of those who hold this view of industrial relations the Task and Individual Needs circles do not touch each other: there is no community of interest. Speaking at a conference in 1964, the Union leader Frank Cousins put this case bluntly: 'We will not resolve our problems if we think we have a common purpose: we have two different purposes.'[1]

We must firmly reject this viewpoint as a perceptual distortion of the three-circle model. A much better word to describe the relation between the individual and the common purpose on the one hand and the work community (with its pressures as well as its social benefits) is *tension*, used not in its main current sense of 'being stretched' (although that offers food for thought) as in its technical meaning in physics: 'A constrained condition of the particles of a body when subjected to forces acting in opposite directions away from each other (usually along the body's greatest length), thus tending to draw them apart, *balanced by forces of cohesion holding them together.*'

In philosophical language we could say that in the working situation the individual is both an 'end' in himself and a 'means' towards the common task. These states are obviously not incompatible, and a close philosophical analysis may well disclose that the relationship between them is complex.

The simple and time-honoured distinction between ends and means is a useful one, and it has already found its way into the literature on human relationships within industry. P. Selznick wrote:

'All formal organizations are moulded by forces tangential to their rationally ordered structures and stated goals. Every formal organiza-

136

tion, trade union, political party, army, corporation, etc. attempts to mobilize human and technical resources as means for the achievments of its ends. However, the individuals within the system tend to resist being treated as means. They interact as wholes, bringing to bear their own special problems and purposes. . . . It follows that there will develop an informal structure within the organization which will reflect the spontaneous efforts of individuals and sub-groups to control the conditions of their existence. . . .'[2]

Some of the historical assumptions of the Trade Union Movement are still tenable today. Despite the emergence in this century of a body of legal statutes on employment, it is still largely true that 'the individual contract between an employee and an employer does not reflect a position of equal strength on the two sides'.[3] Traits in the personality of some managers or corporate managements, which can issue orders in ruthless disregard of the individual when task or organization are at stake, have not been so dissipated that the protective function of Trade Unions is no longer necessary. You cannot legislate against original sin. As the Trade Union Congress in 1966 wryly put it: 'benevolence is not a universal characteristic'.

In the widely-quoted definition of the Webbs, a Trade Union is 'a continuous association of wage earners for the purpose of improving the conditions of their working lives'. As we have noted, this purpose can be refracted into two major aims, one defensive and the other offensive. In turn these aims can be broken down into more specific objectives. The objectives, which are set more concretely in a given social and political context, will arouse much more debate. Not all will concur that any one given objective necessarily flows from the agreed statement of purpose and aims. In *Trade Unionism* (1966),[4] the Trade Union Congress listed ten contemporary objectives:

1. improved terms of employment
2. improved physical environment of work
3. full employment and national prosperity
4. security of employment and income
5. improved social security
6. fair shares in national income and wealth
7. industrial democracy
8. a voice in government
9. improved public and social services
10. public control and planning of industry

Some of these objectives have a direct or implicit reference to politics. In the light of the purpose and aims of Trade Unionism on the one hand and the social structure of British society in the last two centuries on the other, this involvement in politics should not surprise us. But it would be irrelevant to discuss here the political beliefs of the Trade Union Movement or the majority of its members. It would be more instructive to consider the traditional stance of the Trade Unions against our present understanding of the nature of individual needs in the working situation.

If we start from Maslow's categories, it is possible to set out individual needs as follows:

TABLE 7.1. *Illustrating Maslow's Hierachy of Needs*

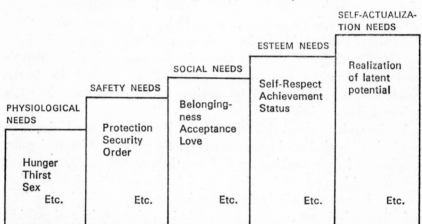

Maslow suggested that the needs shown here towards the left of the diagram are the more powerful ones. If they are threatened a person will abandon the pursuit of the higher (but weaker) needs and concentrate his energies on protecting the satisfaction of his basic needs. Only on the steps of satisfied needs can an advance be made to the higher slopes of human living.

Whether or not this aspect of Maslow's theory is true is open to question. Many people whose basic neds are satiated apparently do not move on to the next level; many others (as Maslow pointed out) choose to meet their higher needs at the cost of their more creaturely wants for food, shelter, security and social life. But we may grant the general case that meeting the basic needs is likely to create conditions for the emergence

138

of higher needs, although this development will not happen by some kind of trigger mechanism or biological necessity.

The role that work plays, or could play, in the discovery and satisfaction of the higher range of needs is a matter for debate. One school declare themselves satisfied for the present with the largely instrumental view of work, which sees it, at best, as a means of getting money to finance 'self-actualization' or self-fulfilment in the private and social worlds of leisure. The other school holds it to be a moral duty to urge changes in jobs and the decision-making practices of companies, believing that what happens in the work situation will influence the psychological health of individuals and will overflow into society at large. Also, through such means as changes in the educational system, they hope to eradicate the traditional and limited class attitudes to work and the expectations from it which sociologists have recorded.

The Trade Union Movement could argue that it has far too much on its agenda without supporting the second school and espousing the rarified higher interests of the Individual *vis-à-vis* the Task and the Organization. Hundreds of thousands of work people are unwillingly and bitterly unemployed, suffering grave physical and psychological deprivations in all their needs. The job security of many thousands of others is explicitly or implicitly threatened by technological change. The wages of those who are employed suffer the steady erosion of rising prices and inflation. Industrial accidents and diseases kill or maim hundreds of bread-winners each day. The Trade Union senior leadership can be forgiven for believing that they are in no position to exert pressure to improve the quality of experience and opportunity in the work situation for those already in secure and reasonably well-paid employment.

Although one can speculate on possible changes as one generation of Trade Union leadership succeeds another and as the general awareness of the non-monetary (or non-instrumental) values in work steadily grows, it is optimistic to expect that more than a few radical Trade Unionists will protest against extremely repetitive, fragmented, or 'meaningless' work, let alone carry the banner in a general movement to improve job interest and discretionary decision-making in all types and levels of employment. Thus we must expect the initiative for small steps in these directions to come from a new managerial leadership tall enough to see the long-term horizon and humble enough to listen attentively to the least important member of the organization.

Not infrequently the less articulate working members will find their spokesman in an elected shop steward, who will be increasingly better educated and trained. It may be helpful to consider briefly the evolution and role of the shop steward in British industry : 'Early workplace spokesmen tended to have limited functions, being mainly concerned with recruiting and maintaining membership, ensuring observance of union rules and reporting back to the union. Shop stewards evolved out of these representative union functions and the actual term was used by the Amalgamated Society of Engineers in the 1870s.'[5]

After rapid growth in the two World Wars there are now over 200 000 shop stewards. Numbers of full-time union officials have not increased at nearly the same rate, and for this reason, as well as a complex of other factors, important negotiations are being taken ever closer to the shop-floor. The Commission on Industrial Relations inquiry on shop stewards in 1971 could conclude :

'We have found little evidence that the steward is innately hostile to management, and much evidence that his lack of co-operation, where it exists, can sometimes be explained by management's failure to accept fully the steward's role.'

The Commission felt that social and economic influences in the general development of industry and society had rendered the role of the shop steward more demanding : 'There is little doubt that the steward's job is becoming more complex, and training is increasingly necessary for him to perform his job properly.' Less than half the shop stewards they interviewed had received any training whatsoever. The committee of the Commission recommended that shop stewards should be given time off with full pay to attend courses. A key question then is, 'What kind of courses?' From the following contribution from F. H. Trenchard, Regional Training Officer in the British Oxygen Company, it is clear that ACL training may have an important part to play in either general courses for shop stewards or as the core for joint conferences with supervisors.

BRITISH OXYGEN : A CASE HISTORY OF ACL AND INDUSTRIAL RELATIONS

&&In 1969, following reorganizations caused by the second phase of a productivity deal, supervisory training needs were looked at. We decided against formal lectures or 'chalk and talk' sessions – and were determined to use maximum participation to ensure learning.

Talking to people in the training field and reading the literature of the day led us to look further into Action-Centred Leadership. Pure

140

ACL was not exactly what we wanted, but the ACL framework could incorporate our own training modules to make up a neat package. A trial course was run successfully, and a programme of residential courses started—each course being critically reviewed and improvements built into the following course programmes.

During November 1969 we suffered a prolonged work-to-rule at one of our major sites. The writer's involvement with supervisors and shop stewards at this site gave him an opportunity to study the relationships between the two. It became obvious that neither the supervisors nor the shop stewards had much idea of each other's role, problems and pressures—each saw the other as someone put there to make things difficult. Observation of this worsening situation highlighted the fact that there were serious training needs in this area—but what kind of training? One had nightmare visions of a shop steward giving a talk on 'My Job as a Shop Steward' to a group of disenchanted supervisors or even a supervisor addressing the Branch Committee on 'My Job as a Supervisor'. These would obviously be useless, except as material for a Giles cartoon.

In handling the work-to-rule negotiation, it became clear that the shop stewards were taking a strong leadership role—and the idea of leadership training for them was considered. But this would not really help the relationship problem. A list of subject areas was 'brainstormed' and it was surprising to find that there was nothing in the shop steward training need which was not also in some sense a training need for the supervisors alongside whom the stewards worked.

Based on the success of our ACL framework for Supervisory Management Training, we tried to hang our Industrial Relations training requirement on the ACL framework—and it fitted. The framework was the basic principle of leadership, developed to the ACL concept of Task Needs, Group Needs and Individual Needs. The training requirements were mainly in the areas of effective consultation, effective negotiation, communication in all its aspects, disputes procedure, interviewing techniques, problem identification, etc.

Each of these subjects was suitable for tackling along ACL lines, because in each a Task Need, Group Maintenance Needs and Individual Needs could be identified.

It was decided that maximum benefit would be gained from a combined shop steward and supervisor course, and that the 'pairs' attending should be those normally consulting together in their working life. Several possible problem areas were identified :

141

- The stewards might reject training by 'management'.
- There would be various levels of comprehension.
- The stewards might use the course to 'compare notes'.
- The Unions would not agree to stewards attending the course.
- There was a risk of 'showing up' a person of lower academic ability in front of the course members.
- The stewards were more experienced and skilled in some areas, e.g., negotion, than the supervisors.
- Several stewards had already received Industrial Relations training from their Union.

Fears were expressed that 'we may be doing a dangerous thing' by putting on this course. Naturally, we had to consider the risks, but my conviction was that the problems, if they existed, were overstated. It was decided to run one course on a trial basis, with a prompt follow-up to validate results.

In April 1970 Course No 1 was held, at an hotel, attended by nine first-line supervisors and nine shop stewards with whom they responded. The course was led jointly by myself and by an adviser from The Industrial Society to give an impartial view. We also invited a full-time official from the Transport and General Workers Union to speak on the first morning on his role in relation to shop stewards. This official gave a short talk into which he deliberately injected some provocative remarks – provocative to both supervisors and shop stewards. This stimulated questions and material which could be developed during the course. There was no script for this talk, and no constraints on the speaker—he was given a subject title and was asked to be provocative.

By the afternoon of the first day some of the suspicion started to clear and some really good participation developed. At about this time there were signs that we had made a blunder in the course make-up. The newly appointed supervisors and the shop stewards were so close together in their interests, that they quickly gelled together into one group—with the Company as the 'other side'.

Thus the first lesson learnt was that we should take a diagonal slice of supervisors, from newly appointed supervisors to experienced works managers, and a diagonal slice of shop stewards, from newly elected stewards to experienced Branch officials. This was done on subsequent courses with great success.

The problem of how to give common training material in a way which would be acceptable to both parties was dealt with in syndicates. For the only time on the course the two groups were separated into a syndicate of stewards and a syndicate of supervisors. The task set was for each group to draw a model showing the pressures on the other group. In a report-back session a spokesman presented a flip chart of his syndicate's work for comment by the course as a whole.

Figure 7.2 and Figure 7.3 show diagrams as produced on one of the courses.

From these models we related common factors and were able to

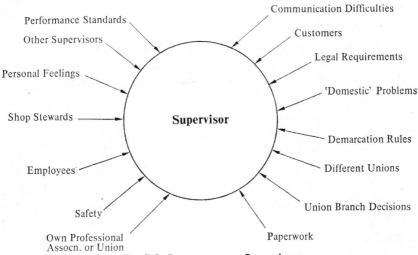

Fig. 7.2. *Pressures on a Supervisor*

Fig. 7.3. *Pressures on a Shop Steward*

143

get some measure of agreement that there was common ground—and that this could roughly be described as the area of Leadership.

Having established this common ground we were able to progress into the areas of basic behavioural science, and to talk about people and their needs in addition to monetary needs. Leadership exercises were used, sometimes with an uncooperative member planted to try the leader's patience!

The exercises further helped to weld the courses together as a group and we were able to progress into the areas of Joint Consultation, Interview Techniques, Negotiation, Communication, etc, in an excellent atmosphere and with really good cooperation in the role play and case study work.

By day two I would defy anyone to identify the shop stewards or supervisors by their performance. It was obvious that both had watched the tactics of the 'other side' and when put into a 'Management Role' on the course, a steward could most effectively put a management case. One works manager, after a particularly good session role-playing a convenor in a negotiation, was told by his real steward—'You can act as shop steward for us at any time.'

One of the case studies involves the analysis of an industrial dispute, and the events leading up to it. The course members work in three syndicates, each syndicate analysing the actions of one of the key individuals in the dispute—particularly the actions which aggravated the situation and contributed to the eventual withdrawal of labour.

A syndicate spokesman has to report back to the main course, giving his syndicate's analysis under the headings of Task, Group and Individual. A considerable amount of useful and sometimes heated discussion takes place within the syndicates on the basic problems of:

- What *is* the shop steward's Task? (although his Group and Individual Needs can more readily be identified)
- Who are the works manager's Group?
- What is the works manager's Task?

Reasoned minimal tutorial guidance in these areas can help the groups to think in depth about these problems and the resulting discussions can be enlightening for the course members and tutorial staff. It is interesting to hear comments such as 'I hadn't thought of my job in that way before' being voiced by both shop stewards and managers. The fact that leaders frequently have more than one task, and that the task can change with a situation, often comes out at this stage.

144

What is the pay-off of this training and how do we measure it? The pay-off is that people who develop a good working relationship on the course can, and do, take this back into their work environment together. There is a continuing improvement in relationship because the people who trained together, consult, and negotiate together back at work.

The improved relationships, and success in consultation, negotiation, and communication in both directions are observed by senior managers and area personnel staff. The improvement can readily be seen by these outsiders and is often commented on by the course participants themselves, who have received this experience of ACL based training.**"**

CONCLUSION

This chapter had necessarily to be a brief one, because the application of ACL in the field of industrial relations is only just beginning. But it is a development which holds out much hope in every industrialized country. For, if power is moving to the shop floor, it is vital that each shop steward should have the opportunity to think out his own role as a leader in relation to the appointed leadership of manager, supervisor, foreman, and chargehand. Although governments, boards of directors, senior union officials, and even legal judges have all pointed out the need for good leadership in the Trade Union Movement such exhortations do not in themselves bring about change. But training can.

Naturally there are difficulties. Fearful of the charge that they are trying to influence or condition the shop steward into the managerial way of thinking, the directors and managers of many organizations understandably hesitate to broach the possibility of joint conferences or courses, not gainsaying the evidence of their value. Equally, some large Trade Unions are only just beginning to take the initiative in proposing such courses both to management and to their shop stewards. It is easy to rest content with training for shop stewards which only deals with such matters as laws and procedures, and does not get to the heart of the matter. In order to achieve this clarity of intention or purpose, with its attendant material, social, and psychological benefits, it may be helpful to use the three-circle model and explore the nature and practice of leadership, as the British Oxygen case history illustrates. It is certainly necessary to mount (by whatever initiating process) joint shop steward and supervisor conferences.

These convictions do not rest only on my own reflections on the three-circle model, but also on many conversations with leaders of trade unions.

From these discussion it became clear that the Trade Union Movement has as much a vested interest as anyone else—perhaps more so—in the development of good leadership at all levels of industry. The present General Secretary of the Trades Union Congress has long recognized the importance of this element. Once, in conversation with the author, he summed up the debate in a graphic sentence he later repeated to the Trades Union Congress: 'What industry needs now is not bosses but leaders.'

REFERENCES AND COMMENTS

1. J. Child, *British Management Thought*, George Allen and Unwin, (1969), 136.
2. P. Selznick, *T.V.A. and the Grass Roots*, University of California Press, 250–1.
3. *Trade Unionism*, Trades Union Congress, (1966), 29.
4. *Ibid.*, 33.
5. *The Training of Shop Stewards*, HMSO, (1971). For the most complete account of the history, role and future development of the shop steward movement, see J. Goodman and T. Whittingham, *Shop Stewards in British Industry*, McGraw-Hill, (1969).

8. Evaluating ACL training

Evaluating ACL training

'The truth is great and shall prevail
When none care whether it prevail or not.'

Coventry Patmore

The problem of evaluation has been raised more than once in the preceding pages : indeed, it is emerging as one of the major problems faced by those engaged in implementing ACL training. Thus it is appropriate that the whole topic of evaluation should now be explored in depth. Such an inquiry into the nature, possibilities, and limitations of judgements about leadership training may prove to be of interest beyond the confines of the particular ACL approach. For a major question mark about evaluation stands against all forms of training, whatever they are called, especially those which march under the broad banner of 'the human side of enterprise'. Are they really worth the time and money spent on them ? Evaluation is a fundamental issue facing all management educators.

Two opposing attitudes or embattled positions are often adopted. Both, in my opinion, are to be avoided at all costs.

The holders of the first set store only upon quantifiable techniques : they will have an objective yardstick to measure change or progress, and nothing else. Managers or trainers who adopt this attitude are looking for some means of establishing with absolute certainty that there is a difference between the trainee's mental or personality state 'before' and 'after' a given piece of training, and that the training itself is responsible for it. Behind this 'scientific' approach there often lies a certain limited philosophy. One manager summed up this attitude for me by roundly declaring : 'What is not quantifiable is not worth considering !' The fact that there is no single 'scientific' criterion can often drive such managers to dismiss training altogether, or at least to restrict it to those areas where it has some measurable effect upon profits or corporate results.

L

Equally questionable are those trainers who never seriously attempt to evaluate training in industry, or abandon the task too easily. They run courses but deny that they can be evaluated. The obvious weakness of this approach is that training of any kind costs time and money, and any manager must be able to justify his use of them, if called into account. Moreover, unless he is seeking to evaluate training as rigorously as he can, he is not going to improve his own methods or the content of his sessions, which is one important aspect of evaluation.

In the introduction to their brief but authoritative book *Evaluation of Management Training* (1970), Peter Warr and his co-authors echo these points in offering three advantages for the trainer in tackling evaluation seriously :

- Evaluation provides the trainer with information that will enable him to increase the effectiveness of later or even current training. Deprived of information about the results of a training sequence, there is no logical way in which the trainer can plan the more effective utilization of his resources.

  It only becomes possible to learn by experience if successes can be distinguished from failure.
- The training department, like all other departments, will be expected to play its part in the achievement of the organization's objectives. If the trainers can demonstrate factually that they are making a genuine contribution to organizational goals, this can lead to an increase in both the standing and influence of the training department within that organization. The amount of support given by other members of the organization will rest largely on the regard they have for the training department staff. So any activity which heightens that regard will ultimately benefit the training function.
- An attempt to build an evaluation scheme into a training programme often entails making some alterations and additions to the original training framework. Our experience has been that these modifications, irrespective of their evaluative purposes, regularly benefit the training in their own right.[1]

The trainer must evaluate if he is to develop, extend, and improve his leadership course, but he must also face the fact that there is no single infallible instrument which he can use to test the effectiveness of the instruction. The only present way out of the dilemma is for him to make a judgement based upon as many semi-reliable criteria as he can safely enlist. Separately they may not give him the answer; taken together they

150

add up to a reliable if rough-and-ready guide to training effectiveness. The resulting judgement will be a *holistic* decision in that it takes account of the whole which is more than the sum of the parts. A seriously negative reading on even one of these imperfect meters or yardsticks, however, should give the tutor or trainer pause for serious thought.

FIVE FACTORS IN EVALUATIVE JUDGEMENT

It is possible to distinguish between the kind of evaluation that aims at determining the level of worthwhileness of a particular form of training, and the sort which aims at what might be called tactical improvements in the contents and methodology of an accepted course.

To some extent the suggested definitions in *The Glossary of Training Terms*[2] (1970) describe these two areas:

Evaluation: 'The measurement of the total value of a training course or programme in social as well as financial terms. Evaluation differs from validation in that it attempts to measure the overall cost-benefit of the scheme, course, or programme and not just the achievement of its laid-down objectives.'

Validation: 'A series of control tests carried out on the training programme designed to ascertain whether it has achieved its aim, i.e., has it been successful in teaching what it set out to teach (internal validation), and judged on the basis of its effectiveness measured against specific yardsticks (such as improvement in quality or quantity of production or reduction in accidents), whether the aim itself was realistically based on training needs (external validation).'

Unfortunately, neither definition includes the all-important point of obtaining the feedback necessary to improve the content and methods of a course as opposed to its 'success' or 'failure'. P. Hesseling[3] has caught the spirit of this latter emphasis much better. Far from being an uninvolved observer and measurer of variables, attitudes, or skills, the evaluator

'enters the training situation in an early stage; he analyses the training needs in the field situation, clarifies training objectives, selects training and evaluation methods, and presents his interpretation of the data . . . in continuous feedback with trainer and trainees . . . the action-oriented evaluator does also try to apply the best methods of measurement and to arrange the most comparable units of analysis,

151

as the 'classical' evaluator, but he is prepared to follow the contingencies of a particular situation. . . . Evaluation becomes . . . a process supporting, tailoring, and intensifying training. It is a continuing, cyclical process. . . .'

In practice all the facets of evaluation are so intertwined, that for my purpose they can be treated under the same headings. There are five major evaluation methods or dials which can be consulted, each with its 'pros' and 'cons'.

1. Course Members' Reactions

This is the most popular method. In its simplest form it consists of asking members to write down or say what they think about a course. Refinements include long and detailed questionnaires, with numerical values attached to the answers, so that one can say, for example, that 67·3 per cent members thought the course 'very good'.

Such questionnaires or the simpler 'reaction sheets' are usually completed at the end of the course. Another refinement is to set a pre-course questionnaire, in the hopes that a change of attitude in individual participants might be measured. The difficulty here is that accuracy demands a fairly precise expectation on the part of the trainer on how the attitudes or views of members *should* change. As the first aim of ACL is not to change people's attitudes in some preconceived direction or to persuade them to accept a certain doctrine, but rather to give each person a chance to think about the leadership aspect of his job, then such 'before' and 'after' comparisons may not be much indication of training effectiveness. But linked questionnaires in this style are well worth further trial and experiment.

Another important development is to ask for member reactions some time after the end of the course—from one to twelve months. When the emotional involvement in the course has faded, it can be argued, people are much more likely to give an objective assessment of their training experience in relation to the needs and responsibilities of their present job.

Certainly one would tend to be suspicious if—after three to six months —a cross-section of those who attended was unable to recall any element of a course, or—more important—to perceive that it had been or would be of any relevance or use in their present or future working life. Worse still would be one's suspicions if the general feeling was, 'Well, I enjoyed the course but now I see that it doesn't work in real life'.

On the other hand, on the analogy of a satisfying and necessary meal

152

being completely digested, all education and training fades from the conscious mind in time: it becomes digested and enters the blood-stream. The further back in time the course attended, the less a member can say with any certainty how it affects his daily life. It exerts its influence, if at all, through the unconscious or depth mind.[4] The trainer has to make the difficult judgement as to whether or not a particular piece of training has sunk into the fertile soil of the unconscious mind, where—like all seeds—it must die to be reborn, and to bear the fruits of effective influence upon action.

The value of post-course evaluation was certainly demonstrated at Sandhurst. In 1962, for example, 140 officer cadets who had completed the old syllabus of lectures on the qualities of leadership were asked to evaluate it shortly before leaving Sandurst: 50 per cent rated it 'little help' or 'no help at all'. By contrast a high proportion of a cross-section sample of 100 young officers, answering a confidential questionnaire *over two years* after leaving Sandhurst, were able to recall the contents of the new functional leadership course and in many instances to give detailed stories of how they had applied it in practice as leaders.[5]

There is a healthy trend towards distrusting the more immediate subjective evaluations. The plain truth is that any form of management training which includes a good deal of audience participation will attract good ratings, even enthusiastic ones. One must seek to learn more about the quality rather than the quantity of the enthusiasm that a participative course has produced. There are still many uncritical managers who equate the popularity of a course with success. The delayed evaluation—either interviewing or asking members to complete a questionnaire some months later—can be a good insurance against a bad course which produces an instant but fast-fading enthusiasm, leaving only a crop of misleading ideas and memories.

A second insurance is never to put all eggs in one basket over the types of questions employed: a good questionnaire should include one or two questions which can be given numerical values and worked out statistically (especially if large numbers of students are involved), but also several 'open' questions which make the course member express what he has learnt, what he still wants to learn, and how he intends to apply it all in the future. A later interview or questionnaire can always check up on how effective he has been in implementing his own programme of change.

Despite the disadvantages, the written evaluation of a course by its members while it is still fresh in their minds remains a solid and reliable method, within recognized limitations and granted certain conditions. Obviously the course organizers must create the essential conditions for honesty : if they show, either overtly or by oblique and perhaps unconscious signs, that they have a heavy 'ego-involvement' in the success or retention of the course, then the evaluators may respond to this perception by trimming their sails to the company wind.

On the other hand, my own experience with over 10 000 officer cadets in the Armed Services, and some thousands of managers and supervisors, has been that—providing you make it clear that you have cleared the decks to receive some broadsides of criticism along with the bouquets— people are surprisingly honest and frank as well as fair in their value judgements on training. They are still the best guides as to whether or not the training has been useful. People are very much better than trainers sometimes imagine at sizing up what they have learnt in relation to their past experience, present commitments, and possible future responsibilities. Yet the brakes of courtesy and innate politeness have to be loosened if one is going to get this kind of objective and useful assessment. Those who doubt the integrity of students to give their honest views are often entertaining, albeit unconsciously, a low or even cynical theory about human nature.

To sum up so far : course evaluation by members is a reliable but not highly accurate measurement of training effectiveness. The right atmosphere must be created, and the questions to be answered must be varied, simple, and straightforward. Where possible, reactions gathered immediately after a course should be supplemented by a questionnaire or interview set some months after the training course.

2. *Superiors' Assessments*

Naturally one would like to know whether a particular form of training has had an effect on what the course member *does* as well as upon his beliefs or attitudes. As we have seen, one method is to ask the persons concerned, either in writing or in interviews. This method has an advantage in that it is also a continuation of training; the interviews serve to reinforce the course, rather like a 'booster' injection.

A second or supplementary method is to ask for the opinion of the person's superior. Has *he* observed any change in the behaviour of the course member, either generally or in some specific area? His evaluation will serve the double function of confirming the value of the course and also establishing the worth of training in the minds of line management, if that still needs to be done.

The superior can be helped to play his part in evaluation by a careful briefing on the aims, content, and methods of the course. The difficulty in this form of assessment, however, which again makes it unreliable if regarded as the sole criterion, is that the superior may not know the person well enough before the course, or not see enough of him afterwards, or simply be not very skilled at observing leadership behaviour. The last two deficiencies may to some extent be remedied, but these limiting factors have to be remembered. One must evaluate the evaluations of the superior.

3. Trainers' Assessments

The whole management of the interwoven process of evaluation rests not least upon the educated intuition of the training manager. If he is worth his salt he should develop his own judgement. The quality of this professional judgement is extremely important. If there was one single and infallible measuring scale then there would be no need for judgement. As outcomes of training cannot be calculated mathematically, they must be judged on the basis of past experience and the imperfect indicators already described. The nature of such judgement is well evoked by some words of Dr M. L. Johnson Abercrombie:

'Thus our reaction to the present bombardment of information involves ignoring some of it, seizing the rest and interpreting it in the light of past experience in order to make as good a guess as possible about what is going to happen. This may be called a process of *judgement*; that is, making a 'decision or conclusion on the basis of indications and probabilities when the facts are not clearly ascertained' (Webster, 1934). We are continually selecting from the information presented, interpreting it with information received in the past, and making predictions about the future.'[5]

Nothing can absolve the trainer from making his own professional judgements about the likely effectiveness of a given course. Among the factors that must be taken into serious consideration is his own reaction to the content and methods of the training. Sometimes his experience will invite caution even when the untutored enthusiasms of line managers are being easily aroused; at other times he will want to give a lead where others hold back, ostensibly waiting for concrete evidence.

There is one tendency which can influence the judgement of the training manager if he is not aware of it. Some psychological experiments suggest that values are affected by choices.[7] In other words, if you decide on Course A rather than Course B, the very act of choice will bias you towards placing a high value on the former and a lower one on the latter. The decision has an effect upon our perception of the discarded possibilities. Thus motives and values not only influence decisions but are influenced by them. Therefore, companies or colleges which have adopted a particular form of training sometimes develop or adopt a value system which vindicates their choice and allows them to justify themselves in rejecting the other possibilities. The training manager needs considerable powers of judgement to assess how far evaluation is being affected by the emotional backwash of the decision to adopt that form of training. It takes moral courage to admit that one has made a mistake, that a form of training introduced into a company by oneself is really rather inadequate, despite the superficial enthusiasms it may have aroused.

Certainly ACL has attracted many favourable reactions from training specialists. As one example, the John Lewis Partnership (Oxford Street) can declare :

ACL as used by us in this retail organization is a *success*—most emphatically. We have found it acceptable by all levels of management. It is flexible and adaptable. We have found that it has helped us meet our training targets and are convinced it has and will help management to become better managers.**

4. Experienced Practitioners' Judgements
One kind of evaluation is the collection or individual opinions of senior practitioners in the given field on the content and methods of a given course. If experienced managers regard the training as sufficiently valuable to warrant the time, money, and effort of all involved this is a good indication. Conversely, if these proven leaders, having observed or participated in the training, are vaguely unhappy or intuitively suspicious about it, then one must pause for thought. It may be that they have sensed something which does not ring true in their experience, although they may not be able to articulate their feelings in public discussion.

Again the trainer must evaluate these reactions, for he will certainly have to live with them. In some cases he may feel justified in discounting a given individual's opinion, but there has to be solid grounds for doing so. He has to find out if there is any basis for the negative reaction. There may be a history of innate conservatism, or simply a lack of intelligence. The opinions of an individual senior leader must therefore be checked against those of others, especially the handful in any organization whose views carry particular weight on account of unique experience or proven good judgement.

These considerations, it may be added, hold good for positive reactions. Senior managers may sometimes discard their good sense in leaning over backwards to be 'with-it' or to be thought progressive. They may sometimes hopelessly exaggerate the differences between the generations, or the situations they faced as young men with those of today, in order to justify their support for an outlandish piece of training which they might well live to regret.

It can, however, be a source of confidence to the trainer if he knows that a majority of senior leaders in his organization thoroughly underwrite his own evaluation of the training in the light of their own practical experience over a lifetime. If they do not it is indeed possible for the less good training manager to rationalize the ensuing indifference or hostility along the lines of dubious versions of Freudian psychology. There is a whole muddled vocabulary which he can call into service, including such useful words as 'threatened', 'manipulation', and 'autocratic'. But such attempts to dismiss the majority evaluation of the senior leadership are at best naïve and at worst positively dishonest.

5. Specialist Opinions

One important form of evaluation not covered in the preceding categories is the judgement of other specialists in relevant or related fields. It should be a sign of confidence and maturity if the inventors of a particular approach to leadership development are willing to allow it to be publicly or privately assessed by independent judges. It does not necessarily follow that the verdicts should be accepted; as with all the other categories this method of evaluation is unreliable if taken by itself. In relation to the other assessment readings, however, it contributes to the overall picture. In the case of ACL one example of such evaluation was a one-day 'Spotlight on ACL', organized by the Association of Teachers of Management in 1970, and led by Professor Tom Lupton, of Manchester Business School. The independence of universities and their primary commitment to finding the truth equips them in some vital respects for a valuable role in adjudicating upon the claims made for management training.

Summary

'The effectiveness of management training at managerial levels is difficult to assess and often impossible.' These realistic words, quoted by Peter Warr and his colleagues from the 1969 Report on *Training and Develop-*

ment of Managers: Further Proposals,[8] sum up accurately the general position over evaluation. But by taking *as a whole* the five individually imperfect measures described above it is possible to reach a tolerably accurate judgement about the likely effectiveness of a particular training approach.

Certainly it is indisputable that if one regards the relationship between trainers and course members as a partnership dedicated to mutual improvement it is possible to go on improving both the content and methods of the training. The function of evaluating is as essential for leaders in the training sphere as in any other; if it is omitted altogether then the quality of the instruction is bound to fall, and the relations of the training manager with his line colleagues and course members could also deteriorate. The problems of evaluation even in the more limited field of course improvement (as opposed to an overall assessment of worthwhileness) are formidable. 'But unless the attempt is made,' the 1969 *Report* concluded, 'useful lessons lessons may go unlearnt, the planning of future programmes may suffer, and valuable resources in terms of managerial time and effort may be wasted.'

SOME NOTES FROM ACL EVALUATORS

The 1970 Survey *The Application of Action-Centred Leadership* revealed that 45 organizations stated that they were evaluating ACL by one or more of the methods outlined generally above, as compared to 19 who were not. The methods actually used are indicated on the following page.

The figures indicate the wide scope for the further employment of evaluative methods which still remains in many organizations. One can only speculate on the reasons (such as pressures of time) which tended to restricted evaluation generally in the middle and late 1960s. All the signs now, however, suggest that the training specialist as well as his parent organization is devoting much more of his skilled attention to evaluating courses. Even so, some of the comments printed in the 1970 Survey already pointed the direction for the wind to blow more strongly :

- The single sheet, simple participants' rating to gauge the immediate impact is complemented by the managers' continued willingness to send people, and ask for further courses.
- The boss and training officer are involved in end-of-course assessment : the consolidated report is circulated to senior managers.

- Participants score various aspects of functional leadership in themselves, and also their team's performance in their work situation.
- The follow-up meeting with participants in a group at least a month after the course discusses how the lessons from the course are being applied on the job.
- Courses are being recommended by senior managers in their staff reviews.
- Course appraisal and discussion with follow-up interview with two of group three months later.

Evaluation Method		Boss	Training Officer	Other
Organizations using	Those Involved: Delegate			
End-of-course assessment sheet				
35	35	—	—	—
Post-course questionnaire				
15	13	4	2	—
Post-course interview				
10	6	9	11	1
Performance appraisal related to course				
11	7	9	9	2
End-of-course discussion				
4	4	3	—	—
Follow-up group discussion				
4	4	1	4	—
Observation of post-course behaviour				
5	—	5	1	—
Continued demand for course				
3	—	3	—	—

- End-of-course assessment together with six-monthly follow-up with individual and his supervisor.
- In-company assessment forms involve the delegate, his immediate boss, the personnel manager, personnel director and the works manager.
- Part of the Training Officer's duties are to visit branches and watch for improvements in handling various situations.
- Follow-up after six months when participants are asked to present a real case study for discussion before divulging the action taken.

The contributors to the present book, mostly writing in 1972, were asked to comment on how they went about evaluating ACL in their organizations. Personally I find the range of their remarks encouraging, especially the involvement of line management in the evaluation and the evidences of 'on-the-job' relevance, which run like themes through the accounts :

Caterpillar Tractor (Newcastle)
    ❝ The three-circle model gives a readily understood and remembered motif and a number of conferees have already reported back on how they have been able to adopt it to solve some of their own work problems. Perhaps one answer as to the worth of ACL lies in the case of one of our older supervisors who wasn't interested in development or training programmes since he had 'heard it all before'. He was finally persuaded by, to use his own words, 'the best example of leadership I have ever experienced', to attend one of the weekends (by a 'persuader' who had been on one earlier). At the end of the weekend he gave the greatest plaudit of the programme we have had. He has found a new faith in the Company's activities.❞

Caterpillar Tractor (Glasgow)
    ❝ Follow-up after the conference is now a feature of our foremen's and supervisors' participation. We believe that, apart from essential feedback on the course itself, we can refresh *managers'* minds of their own particular ACL conference by involving them in this follow-up meeting of their foremen. Briefly, follow-up discussions led by managers concentrate on three questions :

- Can the conference arrangements be improved ?
- What have the delegates learned ?

- What future commitment have they made in relation to their practical work situation?

The best way to analyse the impact of the programme is to list some of the comments made by conferees:

- I liked the interesting way the subject was presented, and being able to participate so fully.
- The motivation session put into perspective for me all the theory I have assimilated over the past years.
- It gave us a chance to meet more intimately with colleagues and work together over common tasks. We will certainly co-operate more fully in our daily work.
- I met Harry. . . . Previously he had only been a voice at the end of a telephone. We now know each other much better and will certainly co-operate towards achieving answers to our daily problems. **"**

The Post Office
" The real crunch is whether or not the training helps supervisors to be more effective in their work situation and its success and relevance must be viewed in these terms. Its general success is such that a National Supervisory Training Centre has been established at Coryton House in Cardiff. This delightful old house is being adapted and equipped with the most modern training equipment and over 100 students, in addition to the experimental groups, have been given the new training. A specially selected and trained team has been formed to run, monitor, control, evaluate, and develop supervisory training in the Postal Business.

The particular success has been that over 90 per cent of the students so far evaluated have done something as a result of their training upon return to their work unit. Perhaps a word about our method of evaluation. Techniques, which we are still developing, fall into three main categories:

- Pre-course knowledge testing.
- Course/session reaction testing.
- Post training evaluation.

The pre-course knowledge and on-course reaction testing is based primarily on the use of questionnaires. They are used variously to test reaction to particular sessions using semantic scales to determine levels of, for example, Interest, Knowledge Gained, On-Job Application, Relevance to Job, etc. These are supplemented by another questionnaire, completed about two weeks after students have returned to their units, requiring more information on the course generally. All questionnaires are 'anonymous' in order to eliminate inhibitions; they have been designed to that end by a staff member specially qualified both academically and through experience.

Post-course evaluation consists of a combination of :

(a) A questionnaire sent to students a minimum of three months after training. This is designed to complement the immediate information gained from on-course and post-course questionnaires.

(b) Reassembly of a student group three to four months after the course to discover whether they had been able to use the course material and what they considered were the weaknesses of training when practical application was attempted.

These reassemblies have proved to be valuable and effective. However, they are costly and somewhat difficult to arrange, and to replace them we are launching a series of follow-up visits to talk to the ex-students and their managers. The visits will be on a random basis and will serve the prime function of evaluation together with a continued monitoring of training needs. We are also considering a further development. It is intended that each potential student and his boss will identify an everyday problem which exists in his work section, bring it with him to the course and tackle it upon return. We are hoping that this concept will allow us to evaluate effectiveness and to limit the extraneous factors which could cloud the evaluation. The following are some particular examples of the application of the training :

- *Student A* went back to a work situation in charge of a planning team with the objective of reviewing the labour force in a particular section. He had little experience of that particular work area or the people in the team but succeeded in creating a cohesive group working towards a common objective, and reduced the cost of labour by an amount exceeding £6000. Both he and his own manager attribute the approach and success of the project largely to the techniques and skills acquired during his training period.

- *Student B* was able to establish a link between an increasing rate of error at a group of Post Office counters and the rotation of the supervisors. It should be explained that supervisors in the Postal Business move from job to job at pre-determined periods. The only common link between all the units examined was the frequency of this rotation. The greater the rotation of the supervisor the higher the rate of error. This concept is very much in line with concentration on Task needs at the expense of Group and Individual needs. This study is currently being validated and if proven could prove significant as far as the Postal Business is concerned.

- *Student C* was a low contributor during the training period and displayed a lack of confidence in dealing with people—particularly those at management level within his work unit. Yet he developed a number of ideas upon return to his unit which he attempted to implement. He succeeded in implementing a number of measures designed to improve work processes together with reducing working group frustration within his section. What was significant about this success was the way in which he convinced management of the need for change. The student attributed his whole success as a result of his training experience. His success revealed his capabilities *to himself*; in short, training increased this supervisor's confidence.

Informal feedback (reports and letters from students and line managers) indicate that there is a definite, although not measurable at this stage, behavioural change. Students are showing a greater awareness of the effect of behaviour and attitudes in relation to people and the way they do their work.

Whitbread

❝A positive attempt has been made to assess this training. Two parts of the assessment have been completed; the first immediately after the course and the second between six to nine months later at follow-up meetings when course members were asked to complete an assessment form showing the extent to which the course had been of use to them in their work. The assessment will be completed by asking the managers of course members to report on the effect of the course as reflected by present performance.

It was sobering to find that the overall rating of the course dropped by some 30 per cent between the first assessment made in a euphoric state at the end of the course and the second assessment made months later. Both assessments, however, showed that the programme had proved to be relevant to the working life of the course members and that the specific subject matter of the course had made the theory easy to grasp.❞

Hoover

66 Comments refer to ACL as 'absorbing and valuable', 'highly participative'. A number of course members indicated that they had found at last some tangible methods of analysing and improving their own performance. ACL helped participants to be more objective and perceptive in the understanding of the behaviour of other people. It creates a strong climate in which managers and supervisors who may previously have been sceptical become willingly involved in a new learning situation.

Used to create a better learning climate there is no doubt that ACL has been successful. It is entertaining and enjoyable but that in itself is not enough to justify its use. Long-term follow-up indicates that not only is the learning *effective*, that is, the material learned is remembered, but also much of the subject matter is applied in the real work situation.

Not having used ACL training in isolation it is difficult to make an objective assessment of its effectiveness. However, all the indications from trainees and their superiors are that the course is useful in a practical way. 99

Kalamazoo

66 As a Company, we are conscious of and have faith in the value of effective training; as a result, all the managers concerned in the ACL course have received formal training both inside and outside the company during their working life. Their subjective reactions to this course were therefore encouraging : 'the best and most useful course I have been on', and 'stimulating'. This is a poor way to judge the effects of a course, but, like many companies, we have been unsuccessfully trying to find a really satisfactory way of measuring the effectiveness of management training.

However, we have seen changes of attitude which we feel can be fairly attributed to the experience of managers on the ACL course. There is an increased awareness of the need to communicate the task to the whole working group and to get their involvement. At the sales branch level managers have been in the habit of holding meetings with their salesmen once a week to discuss new sales approaches and current advertising campaigns. Since the course a new pattern of meetings is beginning to emerge. There is more inclination among branch managers to use the individual skills of their subordinates, for example, to show how they have been successful in a particular sales approach, or

164

to explain a more complex system to their fellow salesmen. Also we are seeing more frequent inclusion of branch secretarial staff at these meetings. These people provide vital support for the salesmen, but have not been brought fully into the team before this.

In other areas managers have started to pay more attention to the contribution their teams can make. The advertising manager has seen a marked improvement in the speed and quality of work of the women in his department (who spend their days enveloping our direct mail campaigns), since he adopted a policy of telling them more about what the enclosures were, what they were aimed to achieve, and giving them feedback information on the results of the campaign. In our Customer Relations Department a joint decision by the working group has provided a solution to a long-standing problem, which has made the department more effective and cut its size by one person.

Most important of all from our point of view, we are starting to see targets agreed with our managers which relate to two important areas of their job—the development of individuals, and the building of a working team. Before the ACL course our managers tended to think simply in terms of task targets. So much more can be achieved if we can get managers more concerned with getting good performances out of their subordinates. Targets of the kind we are now starting to see seem more likely to us to bring real improvements in management performance and task achievement.

Two other results from the ACL course which are rather less easy to define are firstly, the general improvement in management atmosphere and communication, which will have come as much from the mixing of managers as from the course content itself, and secondly, the improved knowledge of each other that the two new line managers who ran the course, and their subordinates have achieved.

As we have said before, we do not see this as a one-off operation. We expect to have a continuous programme of training for all managers, and to give them at least an annual shot in the arm of these two intimately related (in our view) basic aspects of management—Action-Centred Leadership and Target Setting. We are slowly establishing a comprehensive management development course through which all managers will proceed gradually during their career with us.

We believe that target setting is a fundamental part of the leader's job. If, therefore, one tries to introduce the ACL concept effectively into a company, it is inevitable that managers will demand that their task (i.e., results, responsibilities, etc) be clearly defined, where this has not already been done. We may, therefore, be involved in much more than making managers aware of the functions of a leader. Really effective results from ACL courses may also require a fundamental re-examination and decision about what each manager is really there to achieve.**

Manchester Fire Brigade
The Manchester Fire Brigade feels that real progress is being made towards a clearer understanding between men and officers (shop-floor and line management). There is an urge to measure the content of daily routines, establish objectives and set about achieving them. It is not concerned with profitability or production but it is concerned with creating interest and producing greater job satisfaction. Whatever success is achieved will be to the credit of junior management and, in the long term, to the future management of the Brigade.

Conclusion
These comments illustrate the twin aims of evaluation : to improve the content and methods of courses, and to justify the adoption or development of a given form of training within a specific organization. The reader may also analyse them, if he cares to, into the five categories or factors listed in the general section, factors which taken together can provide the basis for sound judgement in management training.

We should not be too hasty in dividing these general factors and the quoted comments into 'subjective' and 'objective'. Striving for objective truth is a necessary activity, but that includes being objective about the subjective reactions of oneself as well as others, just as a theatre critic must read the meters of his own varied personal reactions. Being objective, however, implies taking a disinterested stance, and looking upon one's own interest or enthusiasm as a personal response until it is shown to be shared by others and confirmed by some concrete results in the three overlapping areas defined by the trefoil model. Then these changes have to be weighed against the cost of the training in terms of time and money.

As a corollary one would expect greater changes to follow longer courses, if they were to be judged cost effective. After all, the ACL course in its original form is two days; three at the most. Beyond that time span it becomes an integrating framework for a more general study of the human factors in organizational working life. But there is no evidence known to me that longer training courses in the leadership area produces substantially better results by themselves. In other words, the way to im-

166

prove tangible results may not be to lengthen the course but to improve the overall structure and ethos of the organization, the involvement of all levels of management in training and its appraisal and to develop an educational strategy which defines and discusses training needs before the course and includes such methods as project work in the follow-up period.

Consequently it is never enough to evaluate any one course (although that must be done as rigorously as possible). To secure a just estimate one must also look at the total approach to management development in a given organization. Thus we should perhaps evaluate those who use ACL as well as the course itself. Granted that both the strategy and the tactical expertise of the training department or function is sound, there is plenty of evidence that ACL is doing a good job in highlighting and developing the unused leadership potential latent in most of us and present in vast reservoirs in the organizations in which we serve. Indeed it may be that ACL will mark a breakthrough in the general problem of evaluating training in the human dimension of management. Be that as it may, the rapid spread of ACL has rested upon positive and varied attempts to evaluate its effectiveness.

REFERENCES AND COMMENTS

1. P. Warr, M. Bird and N. Rackham, *Evaluation of Management Training*, Gower Press, (1970), 9–10.
2. *Glossary of Training Terms*, HMSO, (1967).
3. P. Hesseling, *Evaluation of Management Training in Some European Countries*, (1970), 3.
4. For a discussion of the depth mind and its part in daily decisions, see J. Adair, *Training for Decisions*, Macdonald, (1971).
5. See Appendix C, 'Post-Sandhurst Evaluations', J. Adair, *Training for Leadership*, Macdonald, (1968), 145–9.
6. M. L. Johnson Abercrombie, *The Anatomy of Judgement*, Penguin, (1960), 14.
7. V. H. Vroom, *Work and Motivation, John Wiley*, (1964), 85–7.
8. A report of the Management Training and Development Committee of the Central Training Council, London, Her Majesty's Stationery Office, (1969).

9. ACL in perspective

ACL in perspective

This book has contained a review and discussion of the development of Action-Centred Leadership training since 1967. In the accelerated progress of management education in the last two decades six years is a long time. It is also possible, although hazardous, to attempt to identify some of the characteristics of ACL against the background of a particular social and industrial situation which have given it such an impetus.

First, the concept of leadership itself has proved capable of forming a bridge of understanding between senior management and the training specialist. Senior managers had been for the most part educated and passed their formative years before the Second World War, and not a few had then spent up to five years in the Armed Services. Thus, a method of training which focused on leadership and bore the seal of acceptance by Sandhurst would be likely to have some appeal. The training manager, for his part, faced the problem of presenting the so-called behavioural sciences in a form in which they could be understood and used by practising managers, who had traditionally distrusted anything smacking of an academic flavour. With its relative freedom from jargon, its recognition of the importance of leadership qualities and its sound footing in the fields of psychology and social psychology, ACL has provided an early meeting point between these more veteran senior managers and their younger training specialists.

Secondly, the ACL hallmarks of simplicity, brevity, participation, and its practical orientation, taken together have a firm appeal. Other forms of training in the human field have possessed one or two of those characteristics, but ACL has combined within a short compass of time its simple (but not superficial) set of concepts embracing the essentials of needs, functions, and factors in sharing leadership, the 'learning by discovery' method and an action-centred reference. It is obvious that these elements,

171

drawn together into a harmonious single approach, have had an attractiveness for many organizations, and still do.

Thirdly, other developments in management theory and practice have converged into consensus on the necessity of good leadership. As far back as 1955, in *The Practice of Management*, Peter Drucker had repeatedly emphasized the need for good leadership in management. Fifteen years later, John Humble could conclude his wide-ranging *Management By Objectives In Action* by declaring,

'Certainly, all the evidence shows that, in practice, MBO cannot flourish without this sustained leadership and example.'

It has also become clear that alterations in job content to allow for natural motivation along the lines advocated by Professor Herzberg can never efface the continuing need for leadership; indeed such changes depend for their existence and ultimate value upon the resolve and considered ethics of the leadership in that organization. The later writings of both A. H. Maslow and Douglas McGregor, published in the closing years of the 1960s, disclosed their dissatisfaction with the watered-down notions of leadership prevalent in much of the American social psychological and management publications of their day, and their perceptive remarks served as further signposts for the convergence of attention and interest on the character and practices of good leaders.

Fourthly, from its earliest days there has always been an emphasis on evaluation in ACL training. Historically the introduction of a series measuring devices, such as questionnaires, led the military staff at Sandhurst to introduce Functional Leadership courses in the first place, and later to apply this approach to Field Leadership Training. Thus before the training became more widely available in the form of ACL each of its seven sessions had been evaluated in writing by approximately 5000 officer cadets in the Army and Royal Air Force, besides by a large number of managers and supervisors. Most of those adopting ACL have also shared or taken over this conviction in the necessity of evaluating, however difficult it is to do so, and their findings have undoubtedly helped ACL to be accepted by other organizations.

Fifthly, Functional Leadership was developed in a 'public service' organization, by army officers and myself, then a civil servant. It was taken up by The Industrial Society, a non-profit-making body serving a membership which is in itself a spectrum of national and international organizational life. Consequently ACL could be adopted at a relatively inexpensive cost. Besides this non-profit-making character, or in relation

172

to it, ACL has always been an 'open book' : there are no trade secrets withheld from prior examinations or complicated initiation rites for training officers. The theory and methods which make it up have always been open to public scrutiny and critical comment.

Some of these factors will doubtless fade into the background in the next ten years. For example, senior management will tend to be more thoroughly informed about the 'behavioural sciences', through reading or educational courses of varying lengths. Likewise trainers will themselves become more sophisticated in the best sense of that word. Will ACL remain on the scene?

The 'feedback' of information from those who are in the front line of management education suggests an overwhelmingly affirmative answer to that question. There are a number of reasons. In the first place there is a rapidly expanding base of those who ask for leadership training or are judged to be suitable for it. Increasingly companies are turning their attention towards the training needs of foremen and chargehands and their equivalents at one end of the spectrum. At the other end there is a steady trend towards undertaking the major part of management development on an in-company or in-service basis (while still allowing those legendary 'high-fliers' to fold their wings briefly in the ivory towers). At board of directors level, as well as immediately below it, ACL in suitably modified form in these in-company programmes is a way of stimulating common thought and action and perhaps that much rarer commodity—vision.

Also, the proof of the pudding is in the eating, and the users of ACL have found, as I have myself, that the value of the three-circles model becomes, if anything, more apparent the more one expounds it or puts it to work. Good models are so few, yet their visual portrayal of a complicated truth in an elegant two-dimensional diagram can do so much to aid learning. No model can be perfect or definitive, but it looks as if the three-circles has 'a life beyond life' as an integrating framework for a great deal of the relevant research in the human aspects of management. Indeed it helps to define the meaning of relevance in this context.

Nor is there any sign that the *participative* teaching methods of ACL (in common with other approaches) will prove less attractive. 'What I hear, I forget; what I see, I remember; what I do, I know.' Indeed it is likely that the flexibility of methods displayed in the so-called ACL package are becoming much more widespread, and this fact has implications for the training of the trainers. In his review in *The Times* of a National Economic and Development Organization Report on *Education for Management: A Study of Resources* (1972), Robert Jones suggested that

> 'although the management educational sector has responded in evolving empirically new forms of teaching to put over its subject, it has so far failed to develop a satisfactory framework through which such skills can be taught. The management teacher not only requires a depth of knowledge of his subject: he needs a better and different grounding in teaching methods than most of his university colleagues.'

The fact that ACL takes seriously the task area of organizational life, and is willing to submit to the touchstone of results, is also likely to commend it to managers in the coming decade. For all organizations are in the grip of rising costs, and all training bears a price tag in terms of time and money. Although it would be fatal if short-term measurements were allowed to overshadow completely the long-term investment in people which any education or training worth its salt implies, the art of management development in the middle and late 1970s will increasingly lie in the ability to combine both short- and long-term results in a balance. Such a balance can only be achieved by the judgements and skills of trainer and learner working together in harness.

At least some of the seeds of the future lie in the present. Thus it is tempting to speculate on possible developments in Action-Centred Leadership.

On the research front, in terms of the content of ACL, I should personally not be surprised to see much more academic work done on the qualities approach to leadership. In a sense the seeds of these possible studies are already present in a disguised and muted form among the contemporary writings on leadership styles. Although I believe that the language employed about leadership styles is too limited, too imprecise and too awash with unconsidered value assumptions to be of much present use, yet the intention behind it—to restore the leader's personality and character back into the picture—is surely a sound one. Instead of attempting to identify single qualities, however, in the steps of the older traditional traits approach, we might now see research into the holistic patterns formed by qualities, in which each characteristic influencing the other according to their juxtaposition in an integrated whole. Research along these lines can never replace what we have learnt about the dynamic, interactive, or functional nature of leadership, but we may be able to reach a better understanding of the interrelationship of personality and character on the one hand, and leadership role on the other. The very

174

limitation of the word 'role', which is drawn from the theatrical world, is that it can imply that there is no such relationship.

Certainly we shall see an extension of research and reflection on leadership into the realm of value-thinking. The vital and new distinction between Purpose, Aims, and Objectives is especially important at this point. For it is impossible to discuss or clarify Purpose without grasping the nettles of the value judgements implicit in any statement of Purpose. And any valid 'long-term strategy' or 'policy' can only come from a hard consideration of Purpose and Aims in the tilting and shifting context of the kaleidoscope situation in which the organization finds itself.

Moreover, without grasping the organization's Purpose, leaders at the senior level (and increasingly at all levels) will never satisfactorily be able to answer the explicit or implicit question 'Why?' 'Why do it this way rather than another?' Perhaps even 'Why is it worthwhile anyway?' One of the marks of a true leader lies in his ability to give the right answer to this perennial question 'Why?'. And he does this by relating Objectives to Aims, and Aims to Purpose, and *vice versa*. Thus a practical way is opening up for us for understanding what Drucker meant by 'managerial vision'.

As part of a general trend, academic research may also study ACL (and other approaches to training), evaluating them and looking at their relation to organizational change. University-based research workers, for example, are involved in evaluation studies embracing ACL in Reed International and the West Midlands Gas Board. This development is especially to be welcomed, because it promises to buttress present evaluations with more disinterested findings than either the source of a training approach or its users can wholly be trusted to provide, try with honesty though they may.

In addition university (or equivalent) research should illuminate our knowledge of the part which ACL training has played in initiating, sustaining, or developing changes in organizational ethos or climate, its corporate attitudes and activities. Possibly the three-circles model, in a suitably developed form, could come to serve as a kind of 'guidance mechanism' for the complex process of change within any organization.

A more certain trend will be the increasing use of ACL as an integrating core for other types of education and training. Some experimental steps in this direction have been described in chapter six. But there seems to be no reason why, for example, ACL should not provide an introduction to the theoretical study of organizations. The 'classics' of management or organizational studies can all be related together by an imagina-

175

tive use of the three-circle model and its associated cluster of concepts and diagrams. The visual image of the trefoil could serve in the future to give a much needed order and proportion to a whole new wealth of apparently unrelated but undoubtedly significant writings.

Amid these possibilities it is important to remember the advantages to be gained in maintaining the essential *simplicity* of the ACL approach. Let others, members on specific courses, elaborate or adapt it; by so doing they make it their own. But the next generation—or even the next course —should be given the barebones framework once again, so that they too can draw their own implications and propose their own modifications. There may be more permanent additions or references (such as the most useful distinction between Purpose, Aims, and Objectives) but they are likely to be few and far between, and establish their position only slowly.

The fears that leadership training would produce an *élite* in the worst sense, or imply a corresponding low estimate of membership—the contributions of the manager as a subordinate or a 'co-ordinate' (or team member)—have proved to be groundless. We now know that democracy depends on good leadership in every walk of life. That fact, coupled with the established conviction that each person with any talent or potential for leadership should be given the opportunity to develop it as a matter of priority, has drowned these fears.

Moreover, it has become clear that training for leadership is also, para-doxically, the best training for intelligent and effective membership in the variety of working teams, committees, or groups in which the manager will find himself. If he fully understands the responsibilities of leadership and feels secure in his own ability to contribute it in his own situation, it is obviously easier for him to complement and supplement the given leader's own guiding work. Far from creating a gap between leader and group, ACL has only recognized the one which must always be there if the group is to be consistently effective, but it does not over-stress this 'role distance'. The three-circles model, the concept of functions and the clarity over factors in sharing decisions: all these invite a much fuller understanding of effective and enjoyable team membership, which per-haps only good leadership can fully create.

Because of this agenda of unfinished business it is not really possible to place ACL in its historical perspective, nor will it be so for some years to come. As a carefully worked-out form of training it certainly has a lot more mileage in it yet, especially when one considers the growing skill, imagination, and flair with which it now is taught, and the strong evidence that here is a form of training which—both in its content and methods—wins a hearing from an astonishingly wide range of participants in many lands.

Even when that course framework changes by the natural mutation of sessions, as must surely happen to any form of training, there are elements in ACL, such as the three-circle model, which will go on enjoying a life of their own, rather like the second or third stages of a space rocket. In industry, as in society at large, we shall never be able to abandon exploration into the mystery of leadership, nor cease from making ever better attempts to locate and develop it more effectively for the good of humanity.

None of the stages or expansions of Functional Leadership and ACL training, narrated above, could have been achieved without enthusiasm, judgement, and skill on the part of many people. If I may write personally, it has been one of my happiest experiences to work with such people, sharing their intentions and innovations. Perhaps the words of that celebrated minister of the first Queen Elizabeth. Lord Burleigh, may yet speak for us all,

'My service hath been but a piece of my duty, and my vocation hath been too great a reward.'

An ACL Bibliography

The following books and articles refer directly to Functional Leadership or ACL training. References and cross-references to related or contributory writings will be found above in the chapter notes.

BOOKS

John Adair, *Training for Leadership*, Macdonald, (1968).

Edwin P. Smith, *The Manager as a Leader*, The Industrial Society, Notes for Managers **14**, (1969). (Revised edition, 1971.)

Margaret Brown, *The Manager's Guide to the Behavioural Sciences*, The Industrial Society, Notes for Managers 16, (1969). (Revised edition, 1970.)

Arthur Adamson, *The Effective Leader*, Pitman, (1970). (Foreword by John Adair.)

John Adair, *Training for Decisions*, Macdonald, (1971).

M. C. Barnes, A. H. Fogg, C. N. Stephens, and L. G. Titman, *Company Organization: Theory and Practice*, George Allen and Unwin, (1970). (Makes use of the three-circles model in relation to organizational studies.)

David Charles-Edwards, *Leadership Training: A Report on the Application of Action-Centred Leadership*, The Industrial Society, No 171, (1970).

John Adair, *Training for Communication*, Macdonald, (1973).

ARTICLES

John Adair, Learning to Lead in the Army of the Sixties, *British Army Review*, No 18, (1964).

John Adair, Recent Research into Leadership and its Applications, *Leadership Training: Proceedings of a Symposium at the Royal Norwegian Military Academy*, Oslo, (1966).

John Adair, New Trends in Leadership and Management Training, *Journal of the Royal United Service Institution*, **112**, 648 (1967).

> Reprinted: (1) *Military Review* (Professional Journal of the United States Army) **48**, (1968).
>
> (2) *Concepts of Air Force Leadership*, Readings of the United States Air Force ROTC (Air University), (1971).

John Adair, The Development of Leadership, *The Municipal and Public Service Journal*, **75**, 44 (1967).

John Adair, Training for Leadership: The Application of the Functional Approach to Leadership Training, *Personnel Management*, **9**, (1967).

John Adair, Leadership in Management, *Works Management: The Journal of the Institution of Works Managers*, **23**, 10 (1970).

Arthur Adamson, Leadership—Forces Fashion, *Personnel Management*, **9**, (1970).

David Charles-Edwards, Can Leadership be Taught?, *Management in Action*, **1**, 1 (1969).

David Charles-Edwards, The Manager as Leader, *Business Systems*, **12**, (1970).

Lesley Bernstein, The Action-Centred Leader, *Business Management*, **11**, (1969).

Hilary Wilce, Managers Learn How to Lead, *International Management*, **26**, 7 (1971).

R. P. Fitzgerald, P. W. Bracher, and D. Charles-Edwards, A New Brew for Whitbread, *Industrial Society*, **53**, (1971).

Appendix

The Industrial Society is Britain's leading training and advisory body in man-management and industrial relations. The Society is an independent organization providing a wide range of services designed to promote the best use of people at work. They include courses and conferences, in-company or in-service training, advisory visits, information, publications, training filmstrips, and a monthly magazine. The Society specializes in leadership, management-union relations, communication and involvement, conditions of employment and the development of young employees. Its 11 000 member organizations include industrial and commercial companies, central, and local government departments, nationalized industries, educational institutions, employers' associations and trade unions. The following is a representative list of some of the member companies and organizations in the United Kingdom who adopted the ACL approach to leadership training by 1972:

ORGANIZATIONS EMPLOYING ACTION-CENTRED LEADERSHIP TRAINING
APPROACH

Abbey National Building Society
Allied Breweries
BBA Group
BP Chemicals
Barclays Bank
Bass Charrington
Bechtel International
Beechams Group
British European Airways
British Insulated Callender's Cables
British Leyland (Austin Motors)
British Oxygen Company

British Ropes
British Shipping Federation
British Steel Corporation
British Visqueen
Cadbury Schweppes
Caterpillar Tractor
C & J Clark
Chartered Bank
Courtaulds
Daniel Greenaway & Sons
Delta Metal
Evered & Company

Express Dairies
Findus
Fisons
Ford Motor Company
Gallaher
General Motors
Greater London Council
Guest Keen & Nettlefolds
Guinness
HM Dockyard, Portsmouth
HM Prisons Service
Harry Mason & Sons
Hoover
Imperial Chemical Industries
Imperial Tobacco Group
Institute of Health
Institute of Public Administration
John Laing
John Lewis Partnership
J. Sainsbury
John Player & Sons
J. Summers & Sons
Kalamazoo
Kodak
Local Authority Training Board
London Borough of Hillingdon
Mather & Platt
Max Factor
Milk Marketing Board
Monsanto Chemicals

Mullards
National Coal Board
National Westminster Bank
Ocean Port Services
Oxfam
PA Management Consultants
Pasolds
Post Office
Portland Cement
Powell Duffryn
Reed International
Richard Costain
Rio Tinto-Zinc
Rolls-Royce (1971)
Rootes Motors
Scottish and Newcastle Brewers
Sperry Rand
Standard Bank Group
Taylor Woodrow
The Thanet Press
Trebor Sharps
Unilever
United Biscuits
United Dominions Trust
Vauxhall
Volkswagen
W D and H O Wills
W. H. Smith
Whitbread
Wiggins Teape

Further details about adopting ACL training are obtainable from : The Industrial Society, Robert Hyde House, 48 Bryanston Square, London W1H 8AH, Tel : 01–262–2401.

Index

184

185